*March of America Facsimile Series*

*Number 34*

# The Redeemed Captive Returning to Zion

John Williams

# The Redeemed Captive Returning to Zion

*by John Williams*

ANN ARBOR

UNIVERSITY MICROFILMS, INC.

*A Subsidiary of Xerox Corporation*

# Foreword

*The Redeemed Captive returning to Zion*, by John
Williams, a Congregational clergyman, was first published in 1707. Williams, writing with the encouragement of Cotton Mather, described a French and Indian
raid on Deerfield in the Massachusetts colony which
had taken place in 1704 while he was pastor there.
After recounting the horrors of the raid, Williams went
on to relate his and fellow townsmen's sufferings as
prisoners. He intended his narrative to provide edify-
ing examples of Christian fortitude. From his own
point of view, the greatest trial came from attempts by
the French to convert him and the other prisoners to
Catholicism. His account reveals the intensity of feel-
ing about the religious question and the bitterness that
it caused in the Anglo-French rivalry for control of
North America. Williams' book achieved considerable
popularity with the English colonists during the 18th
century and was reprinted numerous times. The edition reproduced here is the sixth, printed in 1795.

In the first terrible moments of the raid on Deerfield,
Williams looked on helplessly while the Indians
slaughtered two of his children. The raiders than put
the town to the torch and compelled their prisoners to
march with them, in the dead of winter, to Canada.
When it became evident that Williams' wife, still weak
from childbirth, could not maintain the pace, one of
the Indians killed her with his hatchet. Many others in
the party succumbed. Through it all, however, Williams' religious faith sustained him. Though near col-

lapse, he finally reached the French settlement of Chambly. There, he said, the French treated him kindly.

Very quickly, he found himself a particular target of the Jesuits, who hoped to convert him to Catholicism or, failing that, to keep him from influencing the other prisoners whom they were also trying to convert. During the two and a half years of his imprisonment in Canada, Williams was transferred from Chambly to Montreal, Quebec, and Chateauviche. Regardless of where he was, however, he could not escape religious coercion from his captors. According to Williams, a superior of the priests "boasted what they would do in Europe; and that we must expect not only in Europe, but in New-England, the establishment of popery." But if the French gloried in the superiority of Catholicism, Williams was no less sure and no less outspoken in his defense of Protestantism. When the French invited him to enter their churches, saying that had they been in New England they would have visited the Protestant churches there, Williams retorted that "the case was far different, for there was nothing...as to matter or manner of worship, but what was according to the word of God, in our churches."

Appended to the narrative is the text of a sermon which Williams preached shortly after his return to Deerfield. An appendix includes material contributed by various persons showing how the town of Deerfield had suffered over the years because of French and Indian attacks. In this edition the appendix brings the story down to 1793. The *Dictionary of American Biography* provides additional information about Williams and his writings. See also R.W.G. Vail, *The Voice of the Old Frontier* (Philadelphia, 1949), pp. 34-35.

The Redeemed Captive
Returning to Zion

THE

*Redeemed Captive returning to* ZION:

OR,

# A FAITHFUL HISTORY

OF

## Remarkable Occurrences

IN THE

CAPTIVITY AND DELIVERANCE

OF

## *Mr*. John Williams,

Minister of the Gospel in DEERFIELD;

Who, in the Desolation which befel that Plantation, by an Incursion of FRENCH and INDIANS, was by them carried away, with his Family and his Neighbourhood, into CANADA.

DRAWN UP BY HIMSELF.

*Annexed to which*, IS A SERMON,

PREACHED BY HIM UPON HIS RETURN.

Also, AN *APPENDIX*,

*By the Rev. Mr*. WILLIAMS, *of* Springfield.

LIKEWISE, AN *APPENDIX*,

*By the Rev. Mr*. TAYLOR, *of* Deerfield.

WITH A CONCLUSION TO THE WHOLE,

*By the Rev. Mr*. PRINCE, *of* Boston.

The Sixth Edition.

Printed by SAMUEL HALL, No. 53, Cornhill, BOSTON.
1795.

*To his* EXCELLENCY

# JOSEPH DUDLEY, Efq.

Captain-General, and Governor in Chief, in and
over her Majefty's Province of the Maffachu-
fetts-Bay in New-England, &c.

SIR,

IT was a fatyrical anfwer, and deeply reproach-
ful to mankind, which the philofopher gave
to that queftion, *What foonest grows old?* Replied,
*Thanks.* The reproach of it would not be fo fenfible, were there not fenfible demonftrations of
the truth of it, in thofe that wear the character of
the ingenuous. Such as are at firft furprifed at,
and feem to have no common relifh of divine
goodnefs, yet too foon lofe the impreffion : They
fang God's praife, but foon forgat his works.
That it fhould be thus with refpect to our benefactors on earth, is contrary to the ingenuity of
human nature ; but tnat our grateful refent-
ments of the fignal favours of Heaven fhould
soon

foon be worn off by time, is, to the laft degree, criminal and unpardonable.

It would be unaccountable ftupidity in me, not to maintain the moft lively and awful fenfe of divine rebukes, which the holy God has feen meet, in fpotlefs fovereignty, to difpenfe to me, my family and people, in delivering us into the hands of thofe that hated us ; who led us into a ftrange land. My foul has thefe ftill in remembrance, and is humbled in me. However, God has given us plentiful occafion to fing of mercy as well as judgment. The wonders of divine mercy, which we have feen in the land of our captivity, and deliverance therefrom, cannot be forgotten without incurring the guilt of the blackeft ingratitude.

To preferve the memory of thefe, it has been thought advifeable to publifh a fhort account of fome of thofe fignal appearances of divine power and goodnefs for us ; hoping it may ferve to excite the praife, faith and hope of all that love God ; and may peculiarly ferve to cherifh a grateful fpirit, and to render the impreffions of God's mighty works indelible on my heart, and on thofe who with me have feen the wonders of the Lord, and tafted of his falvation ; that we may not fall under that heavy charge made againft Ifrael of old, Pfal. lxxviii. 11, 42. *They forgat his works, and the wonders he fhewed them : They remembered not his hand, nor the day that he delivered them from the enemy.*

And

And I cannot, Sir, but think it moſt agreeable to my duty to God, our ſupreme redeemer, to mention your Excellency's name with honour; ſince Heaven has honoured you as the prime in- ſtrument in returning our captivity. Sure I am, the laws of juſtice and gratitude (which are the laws of God) do challenge from us the moſt pub- lick acknowledgments of your uncommon ſym- pathy with us, your children, in our bonds, ex- preſſed in all endearing methods of parental care and tenderneſs. All your people are cheriſhed under your wings, happy in your government, and are obliged to bleſs God for you : And among your people, thoſe who are immediately expoſed to the outrages of the enemy, have peculiarly felt refreſhment from the benign influences of your wiſe and tender conduct ; and are under the moſt ſenſible engagements to acknowledge your Excellency, under God, as the breath of their noſtrils.

Your uncommon ſagacity and prudence, in contriving to looſe the bonds of your captived children ; your unwearied vigour and applica- tion, in purſuing them, to work our deliverance, can never be enough praiſed. It is moſt notori- ous, that nothing was thought too difficult by you to effect this deſign, in that you readily ſent your own ſon, Mr. William Dudley, to undergo the hazards and hardſhips of a tedious voyage, that this affair might be tranſacted with ſucceſs ; which muſt not be forgotten, as an expreſſion of your great ſolicitude and zeal to recover us from the tyranny and oppreſſion of our captivity.

I doubt

A 2

I doubt not but that the God, whom herein you have ſerved, will remember, and glorioūſly reward you ; and may Heaven long preſerve you at our helm, a bleſſing ſo neceſſary for the tranquillity of this province, in this dark and tempeſtuous ſeaſon.   May the beſt of bleſſings, from the Father of Lights, be ſhowered down upon your perſon, family and government ; which ſhall be the prayer of

Your Excellency's moſt humble

obedient, and dutiful ſervant,

JOHN WILLIAMS.

March 3, 1706,7.

THE

# REDEEMED CAPTIVE

RETURNING TO

# ZION.

THE history I am going to write, proves, that days of fasting and prayer, without reformation, will not avail to turn away the anger of God from a professing people ; and yet witnesseth, how very advantageous, gracious supplications are, to prepare particular christians, patiently to suffer the will of God, in very trying publick calamities. For some of us, moved with fear, set apart a day of prayer, to ask of God, either to spare, and save us from the hands of our enemies, or to prepare us to sanctify and honour him in what way soever he should come forth towards us. The places of scripture from whence we were entertained, were Gen. xxxii. 10, 11. *I am not worthy of the least of all the mercies, and of all the truth which thou hast shewed unto thy servant. Deliver me, I pray thee, from the hand of my brother, from the hand of Esau : For I fear him, lest he will come and smite me, and the mother with the children.* [In the forenoon.] And Gen. xxxii. 26.

*And*

*And he said, let me go, for the day breaketh : And*
*he said, I will not let thee go, except thou blefs me.*
[In the afternoon.] From which we were called
upon to fpread the caufes of fear, relating to our
own felves, or families, before God ; as alfo, how
it becomes us, with an undeniable importunity,
to be following God, with earneft prayers for his
blefling, in every condition. And it is very ob-
fervable, how God ordered our prayers, in a peculiar manner, to be going up to him ; to prepare
us, with a right chriftian fpirit, to undergo, and
endure fuffering trials.

Not long after, the holy and righteous God
brought us under great trials, as to our perfons
and families, which put us under a neceffity of
fpreading before him, in a wildernefs, the diftreffing dangers and calamities of our relations ; yea;
that called on us, notwithftanding feeming prefent frowns, to refolve by his grace not to be fent
away without a blefling. Jacob, in wreftling,
has the hollow of his thigh put out of joint ;
and it is faid to him, *Let me go ;* yet he is rather
animated to an heroical, chriftian refolution to
continue earneft for the blefling, than difcouraged
from afking.

ON the twenty-ninth of February, 1703,4,
not long before break of day, the enemy came in
like a flood upon us ; our watch being unfaithful,
an evil, whofe awful effects, in a furprifal of our
fort, fhould befpeak all watchmen to avoid, as
they would not bring the charge of blood upon
themfelves. They came to my houfe in the beginning of the onfet, and by their violent en-
                                        deavours

deavours to break open doors and windows, with
axes and hatchets, awaked me out of sleep ;
on which I leaped out of bed, and running toward
the door, perceived the enemy making their en-
trance into the houſe. I called to awaken two
ſoldiers, in the chamber ; and returned toward
my bed-ſide, for my arms. The enemy immediately brake into the room, I judge to the number of twenty, with painted faces, and hideous
acclamations. I reached up my hands to the
bed-teſter, for my piſtol, uttering a ſhort petition
to God, for everlaſting mercies for me and mine,
on the account of the merits of our glorified Redeemer ; expecting a preſent paſſage through the
valley of the ſhadow of death ; ſaying in myſelf,
as Iſaiah xxxviii. 10, 11. *I ſaid, in the cutting off*
*my days, I ſhall go to the gates of the grave : I am*
*deprived of the reſidue of my years. I ſaid, I ſhall*
*not ſee the Lord, even the Lord, in the land of the*
*living : I ſhall behold man no more with the inhabit-*
*ants of the world.* Taking down my piſtol, I
cocked it, and put it to the breaſt of the firſt Indian who came up ; but my piſtol miſſing fire, I
was ſeized by three Indians, who diſarmed me,
and bound me naked, as I was in my ſhirt, and
ſo I ſtood for near the ſpace of an hour. Binding
me, they told me they would carry me to Quebec. My piſtol miſſing fire was an occaſion of
my life's being preſerved ; ſince which I have
alſo found it profitable to be croſſed in my own
will. The judgment of God did not long ſlum-
ber againſt one of the three which took me, who
was a captain, for by ſun-riſing he received a
mortal ſhot from my next neighbour's houſe ;
who

who oppofed fo great a number of French and
Indians as three hundred, and yet were no more
than feven men in an ungarrifoned houfe.

I cannot relate the diftreffing care I had for
my dear wife, who had lain-in but a few weeks
before, and for my poor children, family, and
chriftian neighbours. The enemy fell to rifling
the houfe, and entered in great numbers into every
room of the houfe. I begged of God to remember mercy in the midft of judgment ; that he
would fo far reftrain their wrath, as to prevent
their murdering of us ; that we might have grace
to glorify his name, whether in life or death ;
and, as I was able, committed our ftate to God.
The enemies who entered the houfe were all of
them Indians and Macquas, infulted over me
a while, holding up hatchets over my head,
threatening to burn all I had ; but yet God, beyond expectation, made us in a great meafure to
be pitied ; for though fome were fo cruel and
barbarous as to take and carry to the door, two
of my children, and murder them, as alfo a negro
woman ; yet they gave me liberty to put on my
clothes, keeping me bound with a cord on one
arm, till I put on my clothes to the other ; and
then changing my cord, they let me drefs myfelf,
and then pinioned me again : Gave liberty to my
dear wife to drefs herfelf, and our children.
About fun an hour high, we were all carried out
of the houfe, for a march; and faw many of the
houfes of my neighbours in flames, perceiving
the whole fort, one houfe excepted, to be taken.
Who can tell what forrows pierced our fouls,
when we faw ourfelves carried away from God's
fanctuary,

fanctuary, to go into a ftrange land, expofed to fo
many trials ? The journey being at leaft three
hundred miles we were to travel ; the fnow up to
the knees, and we never inured to fuch hardfhips
and fatigues ; the place we were to be carried to,
a popifh country. Upon my parting from the
town, they fired my houfe and barn. We were
carried over the river, to the foot of the mountain,
about a mile from my houfe, where we found a
great number of our chriftian neighbours, men,
women and children, to the number of an hundred, nineteen of whom were afterward murdered
by the way, and two ftarved to death, near Cowafs, in a time of great fcarcity or famine, the favages underwent there. When we came to the
foot of the mountain, they took away our fhoes,
and gave us, in the room of them, Indian fhoes,
to prepare us for our travel. Whilft we were
there, the Englifh beat out a company, that re-
mained in the town, and purfued them to the
river, killing and wounding many of them ; but
the body of the army, being alarmed, they repulfed thofe few Englifh that purfued them.

I am not able to give you an account of the
number of the enemy flain ; but I obferved after
this fight, no great infulting mirth, as I expected ; and faw many wounded perfons, and for
feveral days together they buried of their party,
and one of chief note among the Macquas.
The governour of Canada told me, his army had
that fuccefs with the lofs of but eleven men, three
Frenchmen, one of whom was the lieutenant of
the army, five Macquas, and three Indians : But
after my arrival at Quebec, I fpake with an Englifhman,

lifhman, who was taken the laft war, and married there, and of their religion ; who told me,
they loft above forty, and that many were wounded.  I replied, the governour of Canada faid they
loft but eleven men.  He anfwered, it is true,
that there were but eleven killed out-right at the
taking of the fort, but that many others were
wounded, among whom was the enfign of the
French ; but, faid he, they had a fight in the
meadow, and that in both engagements they loft
more than forty.  Some of the foldiers, both
French and Indians, then prefent, told me fo,
(faid he), adding, that the French always endeavour to conceal the number of their flain.

After this, we went up the mountain, and faw
the fmoke of the fires in town, and beheld the
awful defolations of Deerfield :  And before we
marched any farther, they killed a fucking child
of the Englifh.  There were flain by the enemy,
of the inhabitants of our town, to the number of
thirty-eight, befides nine of the neighbouring
towns.  We travelled not far the firft day ; God
made the heathen fo to pity our children, that
though they had feveral wounded perfons of their
own to carry upon their fhoulders for thirty miles,
before they came to the river, yet they carried
our children, incapable of travelling, upon their
fhoulders, and in their arms.  When we came to
our lodging place, the firft night, they dug away
the fnow, and made fome wigwams, cut down
fome of the fmall branches of fpruce trees to lie
down on, and gave the prifoners fomewhat to
eat ; but we had but little appetite.  I was pinioned, and bound down that night, and fo I was
                                        every

every night whilft I was with the army. Some of the enemy who brought drink with them from the town, fell to drinking, and in their drunken fit they killed my negro man, the only dead perfon I either faw at the town, or in the way. In the night an Englifhman made his efcape. In the morning I was called for, and ordered by the general to tell the Englifh, that if any more made their efcape, they would burn the reft of the prifoners. He that took me was unwilling to let me fpeak with any of the prifoners, as we marched; but on the morning of the fecond day, he being appointed to guard the rear, I was put into the hands of my other mafter, who permitted me to fpeak to my wife, when I overtook her, and to walk with her, to help her in her journey. On the way we difcourfed of the happinefs of thofe who had a right to an houfe not made with hands, eternal in the heavens; and God for a father, and friend; as alfo, that it was our reafonable duty, quietly to fubmit to the will of God, and to fay, the will of the Lord be done. My wife told me her ftrength of body began to fail, and that I muft expect to part with her; faying, fhe hoped God would preferve my life, and the life of fome, if not of all of our children, with us; and commended to me, under God, the care of them. She never fpake any difcontented word as to what had befallen us, but with fuitable expreffions juftified God in what had befallen us. We foon made an halt, in which time my chief furviving mafter came up, upon which I was put upon marching with the foremoft, and fo made to take my laft farewell of my dear wife,

B                                              the

the defire of my eyes, and companion in many
mercies and afflictions. Upon our feparation
from each other, we afked for each other, grace
fufficient for what God fhould call us to. After
our being parted from one another, fhe fpent the
few remaining minutes of her ftay in reading the
holy fcriptures ; which fhe was wont perfonally
every day to delight her foul in reading, praying,
meditating of, and over, by herfelf, in her clofet,
over and above what fhe heard out of them in
our family worfhip. I was made to wade over
a fmall river, and fo were all the Englifh, the
water above knee-deep, the ftream very fwift ;
and after that, to travel up a fmall mountain ;
my ftrength was almoft fpent, before I came to
the top of it. No fooner had I overcome the
difficulty of that afcent, but I was permitted to
fit down, and be unburthened of my pack. I fat
pitying thofe who were behind, and intreated my
mafter to let me go down, and help up my wife ;
but he refufed, and would not let me ftir from
him. I afked each of the prifoners (as they
paffed by me) after her, and heard that in paffing
through the abovefaid river, fhe fell down, and
was plunged over head and ears in the water ;
after which fhe travelled not far ; for at the foot
of this mountain, the cruel and blood-thirfty
favage, who took her, flew her with his hatchet,
at one ftroke ; the tidings of which were very
awful ; and yet fuch was the hard heartednefs of
the adverfary, that my tears were reckoned to me
as a reproach. My lofs, and the lofs of my
children, was great ; our hearts were fo filled
with forrow, that nothing but the comfortable

hopes

hopes of her being taken away in mercy to herfelf, from the evils we were to fee, feel, and fuffer
under, (and joined to the affembly of the fpirits
of juft men made perfect, to reft in peace, and
joy unfpeakable, and full of glory, and the good
pleafure of God thus to exercife us), could have
kept us from finking under, at that time. That
fcripture, Job i. 21. *Naked came I out of my
mother's womb, and naked fhall I return thither;
the Lord gave, and the Lord hath taken away, bleffed
be the name of the Lord;* was brought to my mind,
and from it, that an afflicting God was to be
glorified ; with fome other places of fcripture, to
perfuade to a patient bearing my afflictions,

We were again called upon to march, with a
far heavier burden on my fpirits, than on my
back. I begged of God to over-rule, in his providence, that the corpfe of one fo dear to me, and
of one whofe fpirit he had taken to dwell with
him in glory, might meet with a chriftian burial,
and not be left for meat to the fowls of the air,
and beafts of the earth : A mercy that God gra-
cioufly vouchfafed to grant : For God put it into
the hearts of my neighbours to come out as far as
fhe lay, to take up her corpfe, recarry it to the
town, and decently to bury it, foon after. In
our march they killed another fucking infant of
one of my neighbours ; and before night, a girl,
of about eleven years of age. I was made to
mourn at the confideration of my flock's being
fo far a flock of flaughter, many being flain in the
town, and fo many murdered in fo few miles from
the town ; and from fears what we muft yet expect from fuch who delightfully imbrued their
hands

hands in the blood of so many of his people. When we came to our lodging place, an Indian captain from the eastward spake to my master about killing of me, and taking off my scalp. I lifted up my heart to God, to implore his grace and mercy in such a time of need ; and afterwards I told my master, if he intended to kill me, I desired he would let me know of it, assuring him that my death, after a promise of quarter, would bring the guilt of blood upon him. He told me he would not kill me. We laid down and slept, for God sustained and kept us. In the morning we were all called before the chief sachems of the Macquas and Indians, that a more equal distribution might be made of the prisoners among them. At my going from the wigwam, my best clothing was taken away from me. As I came nigh the place appointed, some of the captives met me, and told me, they thought the enemies were going to burn some of us, for they had peeled off the bark from several trees, and acted very strangely. To whom I replied, they could act nothing against us, but as they were permitted of God, and I was persuaded he would prevent such severities. When we came to the wigwam appointed, several of the captives were taken from their former masters, and put into the hands of others : But I was sent again to my two masters, who brought me from my house.

In our fourth day's march, the enemy killed another of my neighbours, who being near the time of travail, was wearied with her journey. When we came to the great river, the enemy took sleighs to draw their wounded, several of

our

our children, and their packs ; and marched a
great pace. I travelled many hours in water
up to the ankles. Near night I was very lame,
having before my travel wrenched my ankle-bone
and finews. I thought, so did others, that I
should not be able to hold out to travel far. I
lifted up my heart to God (my only refuge) to remove my lamenefs, and carry me through with
my children and neighbours, if he judged it beft.
However, I defired God would be with me in
my great change, if he called me by such a death
to glorify him ; and that he would take care of
my children and neighbours, and blefs them ;
and within a little fpace of time, I was well of
my lamenefs, to the joy of my children and
neighbours, that faw so great an alteration in
my travelling.

On the Saturday, the journey was long and
tedious ; we travelled with such fpeed, that four
women were tired, and then flain by them who
led them captive.

On the Sabbath day we refted, and I was permitted to pray and preach to the captives. The
place of fcripture fpoken from, was Lam. i. 18.
*The Lord is righteous, for I have rebelled againft his*
*commandment : Hear, I pray you, all people, and be-*
*hold my forrow : My virgins and my young men are*
*gone into captivity.* The enemy, who faid to us,
fing us one of Zion's fongs, were ready, some of
them, to upbraid us, becaufe our finging was not
fo loud as theirs. When the Macquas and Indians were chief in power, we had this revival in
our bondage ; to join together in the worfhip of
God, and encourage one another to a patient
B 2                                    bearing

bearing the indignation of the Lord, till he should plead our caufe. When we àrrived at New-France we were forbidden praying one with another, or joining together in the fervice of God.

The next day, foon after we marched, we had an alarm ; on which many of the Englifh were bound. I was then near the front, and my maf-ters not with me ; fo I was not bound. This alarm was occafioned by fome Indians fhooting at geefe that flew over them, that put them into a confiderable confternation and fright ; but after they came to underftand they were not purfued by the Englifh, they boafted, that the Englifh would not come out after them, as they had boafted before we began our journey in the morn-ing. They killed this day two women, who were fo faint they could not travel.

The next day, in the morning, before we travelled, one Mary Brooks, a pious young wo-man, came to the wigwam where I was, and told me, fhe defired to blefs God, who had inclined the heart of her mafter to let her come to take her farewell of me. Said fhe, by my falls on the ice yefterday I injured myfelf, caufing a mifcarriage this night, fo that I am not able to travel far ; I know they will kill me to-day ; but (fays fhe) God has (praifed be his name) by his fpirit with his word, ftrengthened me to my laft encounter with death : And mentioned to me fome places of fcripture feafonably fent in for her fupport. And (fays fhe) I am not afraid of death ; I can, through the grace of God, chearfully fubmit to the will of God. Pray for me (faid fhe) at part-

ing,

ing, that God would take me to himself. Accordingly she was killed that day. I mention it
to the end, I may stir up all in their young days,
to improve the death of Christ by faith, to a
giving them an holy boldness in the day of death.

The next day we were made to scatter one
from another into smaller companies ; and one of
my children carried away with Indians belonging
to the eastern parts. At night my master came
to me, with my pistol in his hand, and put it to
my breast, and said, now I will kill you, for (said
he) at your house you would have killed me with
it if you could. But, by the grace of God, I was
not much daunted ; and whatever his intention
might be, God prevented my death.

The next day I was again permitted to pray
with that company of captives with me, and we
allowed to sing a psalm together. After which,
I was taken from all the company of the English,
excepting two children of my neighbours, one of
which, a girl of four years of age, was killed by
her Macqua master, the next morning, the snow
being so deep, when we left the river, that he
could not carry the child and his pack too.

When the Sabbath came, one Indian staid with
me, and a little boy nine years old, whilst the
rest went a hunting. And when I was here, I
thought with myself, that God had now separated
me from the congregation of his people, who
were now in his sanctuary, where he command-
eth the blessing, even life forever ; and made to
bewail my unfruitfulness under, and unthankful-
ness for such a mercy. When my spirit was almost overwhelmed within me, at the considera-
tion

tion of what had paffed over me, and what was
to be expected, I was ready almoft to fink in my
fpirit. But God fpake thofe words with a greater
efficacy than man could fpeak them, for my
ftrengthening and fupport: Pfal. cxviii. 17. *I ſhall
not die, but live : And declare the works of the Lord.*
Pfalm xlii. 11. *Why art thou caſt down, O my ſoul ?
And why art thou diſquieted within me ? Hope thou
in God ; for I ſhall yet praiſe him, who is the health
of my countenance, and my God.* Nehem. i. 8, 9.
*Remember, I beſeech thee, the word that thou com-
mandeſt thy ſervant Moſes, ſaying, if ye tranſgreſs, I
will ſcatter you abroad among the nations : But if ye
turn unto me, and keep my commandments, and do
them ; though there were of you caſt out unto the ut-
termoſt part of the heaven, yet will I gather them
from thence, and will bring them unto the place that
I have choſen, to ſet my name there.* Thefe three
places of fcripture, one after another, by the grace
of God, ftrengthened my hopes, that God would
fo far reftrain the wrath of the adverfary, that the
greateſt number of us left alive, fhould be carried
through fo tedious a journey : That though my
children had no father to take care of them, that
word quieted me to a patient waiting to fee the
end the Lord would make, Jer. xlix. 11. *Leave
thy fatherleſs children, I will preſerve them alive,
and let thy widows truſt in me.* Accordingly God
carried them wonderfully through great difficulties and dangers. My youngeſt daughter, aged
feven years, was carried all the journey, and
looked after with a great deal of tendernefs. My
youngeſt fon, aged four years, was wonderfully
preferved from death ; for though they that carried

ried him, or drawed him on fleighs, were tired
with their journey, yet their favage cruel tempers
were fo over-ruled by God, that they did not kill
him; but in their pity, he was fpared, and others
would take care of him; fo that four times on
the journey he was thus preferved, till at laft he
arrived at Montreal, where a French gentlewoman, pitying the child, redeemed it out of the
hands of the heathen. My fon Samuel, and my
eldeft daughter, were pitied, fo as to be drawn
on fleighs, when unable to travel. And though
they fuffered very much through fcarcity of
food, and tedious journeys, they were carried
through to Montreal. And my fon Stephen,
about eleven years of age, wonderfully preferved
from death, in the famine whereof three Englifh
perfons died, and after eight months brought
into Chamblee.

My mafter returned on the evening of the Sabbath, and told me, he had killed five moofe.
The next day we removed to the place where he
had killed them. We tarried there three days,
till we had roafted and dried the meat. My
mafter made me a pair of fnow-fhoes, for (faid
he) you cannot poffibly travel without, the fnow
being knee-deep. We parted from thence heavy
laden; I travelled with a burden on my back,
with fnow-fhoes, twenty-five miles the firft day
of wearing them; and again the next day till afternoon; and then we came to the French river.
My mafter, at this place, took away my pack,
and drawed the whole load on the ice; but my
bones feemed to be mifplaced, and I unable to
travel with any fpeed. My feet were very fore,
and

and each night I wrung blood out of my stock-
ings, when I pulled them off.   My ſhins alſo
were very ſore, being cut with cruſty ſnow, in the
time of my travelling without ſnow-ſhoes.   But
finding ſome dry oak-leaves, by the river banks,
I put them to my ſhins ; and in once applying of
them, they were healed.   And here my maſter
was very kind to me, would always give me the
beſt he had to eat ; and by the goodneſs of God,
I never wanted a meal's meat, during my captivity ; though ſome of my children and neighbours were greatly wounded, (as I may ſay) with
the arrows of famine and pinching want ; having
for many days nothing but roots to live upon,
and not much of them neither.   My maſter gave
me a piece of a bible ; never diſturbed me in
reading the ſcriptures, or in praying to God.
Many of my neighbours, alſo, found that mercy
in their journey, to have bibles, pſalm books,
catechiſms, and good books, put into their hands,
with liberty to uſe them ; and yet after their arrival at Canada, all poſſible endeavours were uſed
to deprive them of them.   Some of them ſay,
their bibles were demanded by the French prieſts,
and never re-delivered to them, to their great
grief and ſorrow.

My march on the French river was very ſore ;
for fearing a thaw, we travelled a very great
pace ; my feet were ſo bruiſed, and my joints ſo
diſtorted by my travelling in ſnow ſhoes, that I
thought it impoſſible to hold out.   One morning, a little before break of day, my maſter came
and awaked me out of my ſleep, ſaying, ariſe,
pray to God, and eat your breakfaſt, for we muſt

go

go a great way to-day. After prayer, I arose
from my knees, but my feet were so tender,
swoln, bruised, and full of pain, that I could
scarce stand upon them, without holding on the
the wigwam. And when the Indians said, you
must run to-day; I answered, I could not run :
My master pointing out to his hatchet, said to
me, then I must dash out your brains, and take
off your scalp. I said, I suppose then you will do
so, for I am not able to travel with speed. He
sent me away alone, on the ice. About sun half
an hour high, he over-took me, for I had gone
very slowly, not thinking it possible to travel five
miles. When he came up, he called me to run ;
I told him I could go no faster. He passed by
without saying one word more ; so that sometimes I scarce saw any thing of him for an hour
together. I travelled from about break of day
till dark ; never so much as set down at noon to
eat warm victuals ; eating frozen meat, which I
had in my coat pocket, as I travelled. We went
that day two of their day's journey, as they came
down. I judge we went forty or forty-five miles
that day. God wonderfully supported me ; and
so far renewed my strength, that in the afternoon
I was stronger to travel than in the forenoon.
My strength was restored and renewed to admiration. We should never distrust the care and
compassion of God, who can give strength to
them who have no might, and power to them
who are ready to faint.

When we entered on the lake, the ice was very
rough and uneven, which was very grievous to
my feet, that could scarce endure to be set down
on

on the fmooth ice, on the river. I lifted up my cry to God in ejaculatory requefts, that he would take notice of my ftate, and fome way or other relieve me. I had not marched above half a mile, before there fell a moift fnow, about an inch and half deep, that made it very foft for my feet, to pafs over the lake, to the place where my mafter's family was. Wonderful favours in the midft of trying afflictions ! We went a day's journey from the lake, to a fmall company of Indians, who were a hunting ; they were, after their manner, kind to me, and gave me the beft they had, which was moofe-flefh, ground-nuts, and cramberries, but no bread. For three weeks together I eat no bread. After our ftay there, and undergoing difficulties in cutting of wood, and fuffering from loufinefs, having loufy old clothes of foldiers put upon me, when they ftript me of mine, to fell to the French foldiers in the army.

We again began a march for Chamblee ; we ftayed at a branch of the lake, and feafted two or three days on geefe we killed there. After another day's travel, we came to a river where the ice was thawed ; we made a canoe of elm-bark in one day, and arrived on a Saturday near noon, at Chamblee, a fmall village, where is a garrifon and fort of French foldiers.

[*At* CHAMBLEE.]

This village is about fifteen miles from Mont-real. The French were very kind to me. A gentleman of the place took me into his houfe, and to his table ; and lodged me at night on a good feather-bed. The inhabitants and officers were very obliging to me, the little time I ftaid

with

with them, and promifed to write a letter to the
governor in chief, to inform him of my paffing
down the river. Here I faw a girl taken from our
town, and a young man, who informed me, that
the greateft part of the captives were come in,
and that two of my children were at Montreal;
that many of the captives had been in three
weeks before my arrival. Mercy in the midft of
judgment! As we paffed along the river towards
Sorel, we went into a houfe, where was an
Englifh woman of our town, who had been left
among the French in order to her conveyance to
the Indian fort. The French were very kind to
her, and to myfelf, and gave us the beft provifion
they had; and fhe embarked with us, to go down
to St. François fort. When we came down to
the firft inhabited houfe at Sorel, a French woman came to the river fide, and defired us to go
into her houfe; and when we were entered, fhe
compaffioned our ftate, and told us, fhe had in
the laft war been a captive among the Indians,
and therefore was not a little fenfible of our
difficulties. She gave the Indians fomething to
eat in the chimney corner, and fpread a cloth on
the table for us with napkins; which gave fuch
offence to the Indians, that they hafted away,
and would not call in at the fort. But where-
ever we entered into houfes, the French were
very courteous. When we came to St. François
river, we found fome difficulty by reafon of the
ice; and entering into a Frenchman's houfe, he
gave us a loaf of bread, and fome fifh to carry
away with us; but we paffed down the river till
night, and there feven of us fupped on the fifh

C                                        called

called bull-head or pout, and did not eat it up, the fish was so very large.

The next morning we met with such a great quantity of ice, that we were forced to leave our canoe, and travel on land. We went to a French officer's house, who took us into a private room, out of the sight of the Indians, and treated us very courteously. That night we arrived at the fort called St. François ; where we found several poor children, who had been taken from the eastward the summer before ; a sight very affecting, they being in habit very much like Indians, and in manners very much symbolizing with them. At this fort lived two jesuits, one of which was made superiour of the jesuits at Quebec. One of these jesuits met me at the fort gate, and asked me to go into the church, and give God thanks for preserving my life. I told him I would do that in some other place. When the bell rang for evening prayers, he that took me, bid me go ; but I refused. The jesuit came to our wigwam, and prayed a short prayer, and invited me to sup with them, and justified the Indians in what they did against us ; rehearsing some things done by major Walden, above thirty years ago ; and how justly God retaliated them in the last war, and inveighed against us for beginning this war with the Indians : And said, we had before the last winter, and in the winter, been very barbarous and cruel, in burning and killing Indians. I told them, that the Indians, in a very perfidious manner, had committed murders on many of our inhabitants, after the signing articles of peace : And as to what they spake of cruelties,
they

they were undoubtedly falsehoods, for I well knew the English were not approvers of any inhumanity or barbarity towards enemies. They said, an Englishman had killed one of St. Casteen's relations, which occasioned this war ; for, say they, the nations, in a general counsel, had concluded not to engage in the war, on any side, till they themselves were first molested, and then all of them, as one, would engage against them that began a war with them ; and that upon the killing of Casteen's kinsman, a post was dispatched to Canada, to advertise the Macquas, and Indians, that the English had begun a war : On which they gathered up their forces, and that the French joined with them, to come down on the eastern parts ; and that when they came near New-England, several of the eastern Indians told them of the peace made with the English, and the satisfaction given them from the English for that murder. But the Macquas told them, it was now too late ; for they were sent for, and were now come, and would fall on them, if without their consent they made a peace with the English. Said also that a letter was shown them, sent from the governour of Port-Royal, which, he said, was taken in an English ship, being a letter from the queen of England to our governour, writing how she approved his designs to ensnare and deceitfully to seize on the Indians ; so that being enraged from that letter, and being forced, as it were, they began the present war. I told them the letter was a lie, forged by the French.

The next morning the bell rang for mass : My master bid me go to church : I refused : He
threatened

threatened me, and went away in a rage. At noon, the jefuits fent for me to dine with them ; for I eat at their table all the time I was at the fort. And after dinner, they told me, the Indians would not allow of any of their captives ftaying in their wigwams, whilft they were at church ; and were refolved by force and violence to bring us all to church, if we would not go without. I told them it was highly unreafonable fo to impofe upon thofe who were of a contrary religion ; and to force us to be prefent at fuch fervice, as we abhorred, was nothing becoming chriftianity. They replied, they were favages, and would not hearken to reafon, but would have their wills : Said alfo, if they were in New-England themfelves, they would go into their churches, to fee their ways of worfhip. I anfwered, the cafe was far different, for there was nothing (themfelves being judges) as to matter or manner of worfhip, but what was according to the word of God, in our churches ; and therefore it could not be an offence to any man's confcience. But among them, there were idolatrous fuperftitions in worfhip. They faid, Come and fee, and offer us conviction of what is fuperftitious in worfhip. To which I anfwered, That I was not to do evil that good might come on it ; and that forcing in matters of religion was hateful. They anfwered, The Indians were refolved to have it fo, and they could not pacify them without my coming ; and they would engage they fhould offer no force or violence to caufe any compliance with their ceremonies.

The next mafs, my mafter bid me go to church :

church : I objected ; he arose, and forcibly pulled me by my head and shoulders out of the wigwam to the church, which was near the door.
So I went in, and sat down behind the door ;
and there saw a great confusion, instead of any
gospel order ; for one of the jesuits was at
the altar, saying mass in a tongue unknown to
the savages ; and the other, between the altar
and the door, saying and singing prayers among
the Indians at the same time ; and many others
were at the same time saying over their pater
nosters, and Ave Mary, by tale from their chapelit,
or beads on a string.   At our going out, we smil-
ed at their devotion so managed ; which was of-
fensive to them ; for they said we made a derision
of their worship.   When I was here, a certain
savagess died ; one of the jesuits told me she was
a very holy woman, who had not committed one
sin in twelve years.   After a day or two, the
jesuits asked me what I thought of their way, now
I saw it ? I told them, I thought Christ said of
it, as Mark vii. 7, 8, 9. *Howbeit, in vain do they
worship me, teaching for doctrines the commandments
of men.   For laying aside the commandment of God,
ye hold the tradition of men, as the washing of pots
and cups ; and many other such like things ye do.
And he said unto them, Full well ye reject the commandment of God, that ye may keep your own tradition.*   They told me, they were not the commandments of men, but apostolical traditions, of
equal authority with the holy scriptures : And
that after my death, I should bewail my not praying to the Virgin Mary ; and that I should find
the want of her intercession for me with her son ;

judging

judging me to hell for afferting the fcriptures to be a perfect rule of faith : And faid, I abounded in my own fenfe, entertaining explications contrary to the fenfe of the pope, regularly fitting with a general council, explaining fcripture, and making articles of faith. I told them, it was my comfort that Chrift was to be my judge, and not they, at the great day ; and as for their cenfuring and judging me, I was not moved with it.

One day, a certain favagefs, taken prifoner in Philip's war, who had lived at Mr. Buckley's at Weathersfield, called Ruth, who could fpeak Englifh very well, who had been often at my houfe, but was now profelyted to the Romifh faith, came into the wigwam, and with her an Englifh maid, who was taken the laft war, who was dreffed up in Indian apparel, unable to fpeak one word of Englifh, who faid fhe could neither tell her own name, or the name of the place from whence fhe was taken. Thefe two talked in the Indian dialect with my mafter a long time ; after which, my mafter bade me crofs myfelf ; I told him I would not ; he commanded me feveral times, and I as often refufed. Ruth faid, Mr. Williams, you know the fcripture, and therefore act againft your own light ; for you know the fcripture faith, *fervants obey your mafters ;* he is your mafter, and you his fervant. I told her fhe was ignorant, and knew not the meaning of the fcripture, telling her, I was not to difobey the great God to obey any mafter, and that I was ready to fuffer for God, if called thereto : On which fhe talked to my mafter ; I fuppofe fhe interpreted what I faid. My mafter took hold

of

of my hand to force me to crofs myfelf; but I
ftruggled with him, and would not fuffer him to
guide my hand; upon this, he pulled off a crucifix from his own neck, and bade me kifs it;
but I refufed once and again; he told me he
would dafh out my brains with his hatchet if I
refufed. I told him I fhould fooner choofe death
than to fin againft God. Then he ran and
catched up his hatchet, and acted as though he
would have dafhed out my brains. Seeing I
was not moved, he threw down his hatchet, faying he would firft bite off all my nails if I ftill
refufed. I gave him my hand, and told him I
was ready to fuffer; he fet his teeth in my thumb
nail, and gave a gripe with his teeth, and then
faid, *no good minifter, no love God, as bad as the devil;*
and fo left off. I have reafon to blefs God, who
ftrengthened me to withftand. By this he was fo
difcouraged as never more to meddle with me
about my religion. I afked leave of the jefuits
to pray with thofe Englifh of our town who were
with me; but they abfolutely refufed to give us
any permiffion to pray one with another, and did
what they could to prevent our having any difcourfe together.

After a few days, the governour de Vaudreuil,
governour in chief, fent down two men with
letters to the jefuits, defiring them to order my
being fent up to him to Montreal; upon which,
one of the jefuits went with my two mafters, and
took me along with them, as alfo two more of
Deerfield, a man, and his daughter about feven
years of age. When we came to the lake, the
wind was tempeftuous, and contrary to us, fo
that

that they were afraid to go over ; they landed, and kindled a fire, and said they would wait a while to see whether the wind would fall or change. I went afide from the company, among the trees, and fpread our cafe, with the temptations of it, before God, and pleaded that he would order the feafon fo, that we might not go back again, but be furthered on our voyage, that I might have opportunity to fee my children and neighbours, and converfe with them, and know their ftate. When I returned, the wind was more boifterous ; and then a fecond time, and the wind was more fierce. I reflected upon myfelf for my unquiet-nefs, and the want of a refigned will to the will of God. And a third time went and bewailed before God my anxious cares, and the tumultuous workings of my own heart, begged a will fully refigned to the will of God, and thought that by the grace of God I was brought to fay *amen* to whatever God fhould determine. Upon my re-turn to the company, the wind was yet high : The jefuit and my mafter faid, Come, we will go back again to the fort, for there is no likelihood of proceeding in our voyage, for very frequently fuch a wind continues three days, fometimes fix. After it continued fo many hours, I faid to them, The will of the Lord be done ; and the canoe was put again into the river, and we embarked. No fooner had my mafter put me into the canoe, and put off from the fhore, but the wind fell ; and coming into the middle of the river, they faid, We may go over the lake well enough : And fo we did. I promifed, if God gave me opportu-nity, I would ftir up others to glorify God in a

continued

continued perſevering, committing their ſtraits of heart to him. He is a prayer-hearing God, and the ſtormy winds obey him. After we paſſed over the lake, the French, wherever we came, were very compaſſionate to us.

[*At* MONTREAL.]

When I came to Montreal, which was eight weeks after my captivity, the governour de Vaudreuil redeemed me out of the hands of the Indians, gave me good clothing, took me to his table, gave me the uſe of a very good chamber, and was in all reſpects, relating to my outward man, courteous and charitable to admiration. At my firſt entering into his houſe, he ſent for my two children, who were in the city, that I might ſee them ; and promiſed to do what he could to get all my children and neighbours out of the hands of the ſavages. My change of diet, after the difficulties of my journeys, cauſed an alteration in my body : I was phyſicked, blooded, and very tenderly taken care of in my ſickneſs. The governour redeemed my eldeſt daughter out of the hands of the Indians ; and ſhe was carefully tended in the hoſpital, until ſhe was well of her lameneſs ; and by the governour provided for with reſpect, during her ſtay in the country. My youngeſt child was redeemed by a gentlewoman in the city, as the Indians paſſed by. After the Indians had been at their fort, and diſcourſed with the prieſts, they came back, and offered to the gentlewoman a man for the child, alleging that the child could not be profitable to her, but the man would, for he was a weaver, and his ſervice would much advance the deſign ſhe had of mak-

ing

ing cloth : But God over-ruled fo far, that this temptation to the woman prevailed not for an exchange ; for had the child gone to the Indian fort, in an ordinary way it had abode there ftill, as the reft of the children carried thither do. The governour gave orders to certain officers to get the reft of my children out of the hands of the Indians, and as many of my neighbours as they could. After fix weeks, a merchant of the city obtained my eldeft fon, who was taken to live with him. He took a great deal of pains to perfuade the favages to part with him. An Indian came to the city (Sagamore George of Pennicook) from Cowafs, and brought word of my fon Stephen's being near Cowafs, and fome money was put into his hand for his redemption, and a promife of full fatisfaction if he brought him ; but the Indian proved unfaithful, and I never faw my child till a year after.

The governour ordered a prieft to go along with me to fee my youngeft daughter among the Macquas, and endeavour for her ranfom. I went with him ; he was very courteous to me ; and from his parifh, which was near the Macqua fort, he wrote a letter to the jefuit, to defire him to fend my child to fee me, and to fpeak with them who took her, to come along with her. But the jefuit wrote back a letter, That I fhould not be permitted to fpeak with, or fee my child ; and if I came, my labour would be loft ; and that the Macquas would as foon part with their hearts as my child. At my return to the city, I with an heavy heart carried the jefuit's letter to the governour, who, when he read it, was very angry,
and

and endeavoured to comfort me, affuring me I
fhould fee her, and fpeak with her ; and he would
to his utmoft endeavour for her ranfom. Accordingly, he fent to the jefuits, who were in
the city, and bid them improve their intereft for
the obtaining the child. After fome days, he
went with me in his own perfon to the fort.
When we came thither, he difcourfed with the
jefuits ; after which, my child was brought into
the chamber where I was. I was told I might
fpeak with her, but fhould be permitted to fpeak
to no other Englifh perfon there. My child was
about feven years old ; I difcourfed with her
near an hour ; fhe could read very well, and had
not forgotten her catechifm ; and was very de-
firous to be redeemed out of the hands of the Macquas, and bemoaned her ftate among them, telling me how they profaned God's Sabbaths ;
and faid, fhe thought that a few days before they
had been mocking the devil, and that one of the
jefuits ftood and looked on them. I told her,
fhe muft pray to God for his grace every day.
She faid, fhe did as fhe was able, and God helped
her ; but, fays fhe, They force me to fay fome
prayers in latin, but I do not underftand one word
of them ; I hope it will not do me any harm.
I told her, fhe muft be careful fhe did not forget
her catechifm, and the fcriptures fhe had learnt
by heart. She told the captives after I was gone,
as fome of them have fince informed me, almoft
every thing I fpake to her ; and faid, fhe was
much afraid fhe fhould forget her catechifm,
having none to inftruct her. I faw her once, a
few days after, in the city, but had not many
　　　　　　　　　　　　　　　　minutes

minutes of time with her ; but what time I had, I improved to give her the best advice I could. The governour laboured much for her redemption ; at last he had a promise of it, in case he would procure for them an Indian girl in her stead. Accordingly, he sent up the river, some hundreds of leagues, for one ; but it was refused, when offered by the governour. He offered them an hundred pieces of eight for her redemption, but it was refused. His lady went over to beg her from them, but all in vain ; she is there still ; and has forgotten to speak English. Oh ! that all who peruse this history would join in their fervent requests to God, with whom all things are possible, that this poor child, and so many others of our children who have been cast upon God from the womb, and are now outcasts ready to perish, might be gathered from their dispersions, and receive sanctifying grace from God !

When I had discoursed with the child, and was coming out of the fort, one of the jesuits went out of the chamber with me, and some soldiers, to convey me to the canoe. I saw some of my poor neighbours, who stood with longing expectations to see me, and speak with me, and had leave from their savage masters so to do. I was by the jesuit himself thrust along by force, and permitted only to tell them some of their relations (they asked after) were well in the city, and that with a very audible voice ; being not permitted to come near to them. After my return to the city I was very melancholly, for I could not be permitted so much as to pray with the English, who

who dwelt in the fame houfe.    And the Englifh,
who came to fee me, were moft of them put back
by the guard at the door, and not fuffered to come
and fpeak with me.    Sometimes the guard was
fo ftrict that I could fcarce go afide on neceffary
occafions without a repulfe ; and whenever I
went out into the city (a favour the governour
himfelf never refufed when I afked it of him)
there were fpies to watch me, and to obferve
whether I fpake to the Englifh.    Upon which
I told fome of the Englifh, they muft be careful
to call to mind and improve former inftructions,
and endeavour to ftand at a further diftance for a
while, hoping that after a fhort time I fhould
have more liberty of converfing with them.    But
fome fpies, fent out, found on a Sabbath day
more than three (the number we, by their order
publifhed, were not to exceed together) of us in
company, who informed the prieft ; the next day
one of the priefts told me, I had a greater number of the Englifh with me, and that I had fpoken
fomething reflecting on their religion.    I fpake
to the governour, defiring that no forcible means
might be ufed with any of the captives refpect-
ing their religion ; he told me, he allowed no
fuch thing.    I am perfuaded that the governour,
if he might act himfelf, would not have fuffered fuch things to be done as have been done,
and that he never did know of feveral things
acted againft the Englifh.

At my firft coming to Montreal, the governour told me, I fhould be fent home as foon as
captain Battifs was returned, and not before ; and
that I was taken in order to his redemption.

The

The governour fought by all means to divert me from my melancholy forrows, and always fhewed a willingnefs for feeing my children. And one day I told him of my defign of walking into the city ; he pleafantly anfwered, Go with all my heart. His eldeft fon went with me as far as the door, and faw the guard ftop me ; he went in and informed his father, who came to the door and afked, why they affronted the gentleman going out ? They faid, it was their order : But with an angry countenance he faid, his orders were that I fhould not be ftopt. But within a little time I had my orders to go down to Quebec. Another thing fhowing that many things are done without the governour's confent, though his name be ufed to juftify them, (viz.) I afked the prieft, after I had been at Montreal two days, leave to go and fee my youngeft child ; he faid, Whenever you would fee him, tell me, and I will bring him to you ; for, fays he, the governour is not willing you fhould go thither. And yet, not many days after, when we were at dinner, the governour's lady (feeing me fad) fpake to an officer at table, who could fpeak latin, to tell me, that after dinner I fhould go along with them and fee my two children. And accordingly after dinner I was carried to fee them ; and when I came to the houfe, I found three or four Englifh captives, who lived there, and I had leave to difcourfe with them. And not long after, the governour's lady afked me to go along with her to the hofpital, to fee one of my neighbours fick there.

One day one of the jefuits came to the governour,

our, and told the company there, that he never
saw such persons as were taken from Deerfield.
Said he, The Macquas will not suffer any of their
prisoners to abide in their wigwams whilst they
themselves are at mass, but carry them with them
to the church, and they cannot be prevailed with
to fall down on their knees to pray there ; but
no sooner are they returned to their wigwams,
but they fall down on their knees to prayer.   He
said, they could do nothing with the grown persons there ; and they hindred the children's com-
plying.   Whereupon, the jesuits counselled the
Macquas to sell all the grown persons from the
fort ; a stratagem to seduce poor children.   Oh
Lord ! Turn the counsels of these Ahitophels into foolishness, and make the counsels of the
heathen of none effect !

Here I observed, they were wonderfully lifted
up with pride, after the return of captain Mon-
tinug from Northampton, with news of success :
They boasted of their success against New-England.   And they sent out an army, as they said,
of seven hundred men, if I mistake not, two
hundred of whom were French, in company of
which army went several jesuits ; and said, they
would lay desolate all the places on Connecticut
river.   The superiour of the priests told me, their
general was a very prudent and brave commander, of undaunted courage, and doubted not
but they should have great success.   This army
went away in such a boasting, triumphant manner, that I had great hopes God would discover
and disappoint their designs ; our prayers were
not wanting for the blasting such a bloody design.

fign.   The fuperior of the priefts faid to me, do
not flatter yourfelves in hopes of a fhort captivity ; for, faid he, there are two young princes
contending for the kingdom of Spain ; and a
third, that care was to be taken for his eftablifhment on the Englifh throne.   And boafted what
they would do in Europe ; and that we muft expect not only in Europe, but in New-England,
the eftablifhment of popery.   I faid, Glory not,
God can make great changes in a little time, and
revive his own intereft, and yet fave his poor
afflicted people.   Said he, The time for miracles
is paft ; and in the time of the laft war, the king
of France was, as it were, againft all the world,
and yet did very great things ; but now the kingdom of Spain is for him, and the duke of Bavaria, and the duke of Savoy, &c. and fpake in a
lofty manner of great things to be done by them ;
and having the world, as I may fay, in fubjection
to them.

I was fent down to Quebec in company of
governour de Ramfey, governour of Montreal,
and the fuperior of the jefuits, and ordered to live
with one of the council ; from whom I received
many favours for feven weeks.   He told me, it
was the priefts' doings to fend me down before
the governour came down ; and that if I went
much to fee the Englifh, or they came much to
vifit me, I fhould yet certainly be fent away,
where I fhould have no converfe with the Englifh.

[*At* QUEBEC.]

After my coming down to Quebec, I was invited to dine with the jefuits, and to my face they
were civil enough.   But after a few days, a young
gentleman

gentleman came to my chamber, and told me,
that one of the jesuits (after we had done dinner)
made a few distichs of verses, and gave them to
his scholars to translate into French : He shewed
them to me. The import of them was, " That
" the king of France's grand-son had sent out his
" huntsmen, and that they had taken a wolf,
" who was shut up, and now he hopes the sheep
" would be in safety." I knew, at the reading of
them, what he aimed at ; but held my peace, as
though I had been ignorant of the jesuit's intention. Observing this reproaching spirit, I said
in my heart, If God will bless, let men curse if
they please : And I looked to God in Christ, the
great shepherd, to keep his scattered sheep among
so many Romish ravenous wolves, and to remember the reproaches wherewith his holy
name, ordinances, and servants were daily re-
proached. And upon an observation of the time
of these verses being composed, I find that near
the same time the bishop of Canada, with twenty
ecclesiasticks, were taken by the English, as they
were coming from France, and carried into England as prisoners of war.

One Sabbath day morning, I observed many
signs of approaching rain, a great moisture on the
stones of the hearth and chimney jambs. I was
that day invited to dine with the jesuits ; and
when I went up to dinner it began to rain a
small drizzling rain : The superior told me, they
had been praying for rain that morning : And lo,
(says he), it begins to rain. I told him, I could
tell him of many instances of God's hearing our
prayers for rain. However, in the afternoon

D 2 _                                    there

there was a general proceffion of all orders, priefts, jefuits and friars, and the citizens, in great pomp, carrying (as they faid) as an holy relick, one of the bones of St. Paul. The next day I was invited to the priefts' feminary to dinner; Oh, faid they, we went in proceffion yefterday for rain, and fee what a plentiful rain followed. I anfwered, We had been anfwered when praying for rain, when no fuch figns of rain, and the beginnings of rain preceeded, as now with them, before they appointed or began their proceffion, &c. However, they upbraided me, that God did not approve of our religion, in that he difregarded our prayers, and accepted theirs. For (faid they) we heard you had days of fafting and prayer before the fleet came to Quebec; God would not regard your prayers, but heard ours, and almoft in a miraculous way preferved us when affaulted, and refufed to hear your faft-day prayers for your prefervation, but heard ours for your defolation, and our fuccefs. They boafted alfo of their king, and his greatnefs, and fpake of him as though there could be no fettlement in the world but as he pleafed; reviling us as in a low and languifhing cafe, having no king, but being under the government of a Queen: And fpake as though the duke of Bavaria would in a fhort time be emperour. From this day forward God gave them to hear forrowful tidings from Europe: That a war was commenced againft the duke of Savoy, and fo their enemies increafed: Their bifhop taken, and two millions of wealth with him. News every year more diftreffing and impoverifhing to them; and the duke of Bavaria,

fo

fo far from being emperour, that he is difpoffeff-
ed of his dukedom ; and France, fo far from being ftrengthened by Spain, that the kingdom of
Spain was like to be an occafion of the weaken-
ing and impoverifhing their own kingdom ; they
themfelves fo reporting.　And their great army
going againft New-England turned back afham-
ed ; and they difcouraged and difheartened ; and
every year, very exercifing fears and cares, as to
the favages who live up the river.　Before the
return of that army, they told me, We were led
up and down, and fold by the heathen, as fheep
for the flaughter, and they could not devife what
they fhould do with us, we fhould be fo many
prifoners, when the army returned.　The jefuits
told me, it was a great mercy that fo many of our
children were brought to them, and that now,
efpecially fince they were not like fpeedily to be
returned, there was hope of their being brought
over to the Romifh faith.　They would take the
Englifh children, born among them, and againft
the confent of their parents, baptize them.　One
jefuit came to me and afked, whether all the
Englifh at Loret, (a place not far from Quebec,
where the favages lived), were baptized ? I told
him they were.　He faid, if they be not, let me
know of it, that I may baptize them, for fear
they fhould die and be damned, if they died
without baptifm.　Says he, When the favages
went againft you, I charged them to baptize all
children before they killed them ; fuch was my
defire of your eternal falvation, though you were
our enemies.　There was a gentleman called
Monfieur de Beauville, a captain, the brother of
　　　　　　　　　　　　　　　　　the

the lord intendant, who was a good friend to me; and very courteous to all the captives ; he lent me an Englifh bible, and when he went to France, gave it me.

*All means were ufed to feduce poor fouls.*

I was invited one day to dine with one of chief note ; as I was going, I met with the fuperiour of the jefuits coming out of the houfe, and he came in after dinner ; and prefently it was propounded to me, if I would ftay among them, and be of their religion, I fhould have a great and honourable penfion from the king every year. The fuperior of the jefuits turned to me, and faid, 'Sir, 'you have manifefted much grief and forrow for 'your feparation from fo many of your neighbours 'and children ; if you will now comply with this 'offer and propofal, you may have all your child-'ren with you ; and here will be enough for an 'honourable maintenance for you and them.' I anfwered, Sir, if I thought your religion to be true, I would embrace it freely without any fuch offer ; but fo long as I believe it to be what it is, the offer of the whole world is of no more value to me than a blackberry ; and manifefted fuch an abhorrence of this propofal, that I fpeedily went to take my leave and be gone. Oh ! Sir (faid he) fit down, why in fuch a hurry, you are alone in your chamber, divert yourfelf a little longer ; and fell to other difcourfe ; and within half an hour fays again, Sir, I have one thing earneftly to requeft of you, I pray pleafure me ! I faid, let your lordfhip fpeak ; faid he, I pray come down to the palace to-morrow morning, and honour me with your company in my coach to the great church,

church, it being then a faints day.    I anfwered,
Afk me any thing wherein I can ferve you with
a good confcience, and I am ready to gratify you,
but I muft afk your excufe here ;  and immediately went away from him.    Returning unto
my chamber, I gave God thanks for his upholding
of me ;  and alfo made an inquiry with myfelf,
whether I had, by any action, given encouragement for fuch a temptation.

[*At* CHATEAUVICHE.]

Not many days after, and a few days before
governour de Vaudreuil's coming down, I was
fent away, fifteen miles down the river, that I
might not have opportunity of converfe with the
Englifh.   I was courteoufly treated by the French,
and the prieft of that parifh ;  they told me he
was one of the moft learned men in the country ;
he was a very ingenious man, zealous in their
way, but yet very familiar.    I had many difputes
with the priefts who came thither ;  and when
I ufed their own authors to confute fome of their
pofitions, my books, borrowed of them, were
taken away from me, for they faid, I made an ill
ufe of them.    They having, many of them,
boafted of their unity in doctrine and profeffion,
were loth I fhould fhow them, from their own
beft approved authors, as many different opinions
as they could charge againft us.    Here, again, a
gentleman, in the prefence of the old bifhop and
a prieft, offered me his houfe, and whole living,
with affurance of honour, wealth and employ-
ment, if I would embrace their ways.    I told
them, I had an indignation of foul againft fuch
offers on fuch terms, as parting with what was

more valuable than all the world ; alleging, *What is a man profited if he gain the whole world, and lose his own soul ? or what shall a man give in exchange for his soul ?* I was sometimes told, I might have all my children if I would comply, and must never expect to have them on any other terms. I told them, my children were dearer to me than all the world, but I would not deny Christ and his truths for the having of them with me ; I would still put my trust in God, who could perform all things for me.

I am persuaded that the priest of that parish, where I kept, abhorred their sending down the heathen to commit outrages against the English, saying, it was more like committing murders, than managing a war. In my confinement in this parish, I had my undisturbed opportunities to be humbly imploring grace for ourselves, for soul and body, for his protecting presence with New-England, and his disappointing the bloody designs of enemies ; that God would be a little sanctuary to us in a land of captivity, and that our friends in New-England might have grace to make a more thankful and fruitful improvement of the means of grace than we had done ; who, by our neglects, find ourselves out of God's sanctuary.

On the twenty-first of October, 1704, I received some letters from New-England, with an account that many of our neighbours escaped out of the desolations in the fort, and that my dear wife was carried back, and decently buried : And that my eldest son, who was absent in our desolation, was sent to college, and provided for ; which occasioned thanksgiving to God in the midst of afflictions,

afflictions, and caufed prayers, even in Canada, to
be going daily up to Heaven for a bleffing upon
benefactors, fhowing fuch kindnefs to the defolate
and afflicted. The confideration of fuch crafty
defigns to enfnare young ones, and to turn them
from the fimplicity of the gofpel to Romifh fuperftition, was very exercifing ; fometimes they
would tell me my children, fometimes my neighbours, were turned to be of their religion. Some
made it their work to allure poor fouls by flatteries and great promifes, fome threatened, fome
offered abufive carriage to fuch as refufed to go
to church and be prefent at mafs. Some they
induftrioufly contrived to get married among
them. A prieft drew up a compendium of the
Roman catholick faith, and pretended to prove it
by the fcriptures, telling the Englifh, that all
they required was contained in the fcriptures,
which they acknowledged to be the rule of faith
and manners ; but it was by fcriptures horribly
perverted and abufed. I could never come to
the fight of it, (though I often earneftly entreated
a copy of it), until I was on fhipboard, for our
voyage to New-England ; but hearing of it, I
endeavoured to poffefs the Englifh with their
danger of being cheated with fuch a pretence.
I underftood they would tell the Englifh that I
was turned, that they might gain them to change
their religion. Thefe their endeavours to feduce
to popery were very exercifing to me : And in
my folitarinefs I drew up thefe following forrowful, mournful confiderations, though unufed to,
and unfkilful in poetry, yet in a plain ftyle, for
the ufe of fome of the captives, who would fometimes

times make their secret visits to me, which, at
the desire of some of them, are here made publick.

*Some contemplations of the poor and desolate state of
the church at Deerfield.*

THE sorrows of my heart enlarged are,
Whilst I my present state with past compare.
I frequently unto God's house did go,
With christian friends, his praises forth to show.
But now, I solitary sit, both sigh and cry,
Whilst my flock's misery think on do I.
   Many, both old & young, were slain out-right ;
Some, in a bitter season, took their flight.
Some burnt to death, and others stifled were ;
The enemy no sex or age would spare.
The tender children, with their parents sad,
Are carried forth as captives, some unclad.
Some murdered in the way, unburied left,
And some, through famine, were of life bereft.
After a tedious journey, some are sold,
Some kept in heathen hands, all from Christ's fold :
By popish rage, and heath'nish cruelty,
Are banished.   Yea some compell'd to be
Present at mass.   Young children parted are
From parents, and such as instructors were.
Crafty designs are us'd by papists all,
In ignorance of truth, them to inthrall.
Some threat'ned are, unless they will comply,
In heathen's hands again be made to lie.
To some, large promises are made, if they
Will truths renounce, & choose their popish way.
   Oh Lord ! mine eyes on thee shall waiting be,
Till thou again turn our captivity.

Their

Their Romish plots, thou canst confound ; & save
This little flock, this mercy I do crave.
Save us from all our sins, and yet again
Deliver us from them who truth disdain.

　Lord ! for thy mercy sake, thy cov'nant mind ;
And in thy house again, rest let us find.

　So we thy praises forth will shew, and speak
Of all thy wond'rous works, yea we will seek
The advancement of thy great and glorious name,
Thy rich and sovereign grace we will proclaim.


　THE hearts of some were ready to be dis-
couraged and sink, saying, They were out of
sight, and so out of mind. I endeavoured to
persuade them we were not forgotten, that
undoubtedly many prayers were continually going up to heaven for us. Not long after, came
captain Livingston, and Mr. Sheldon, with letters from his excellency our governor to the governour of Canada, about the exchange of prisoners ; which gave a revival to many, and raised
expectations of a return. These visits from New-
England to Canada, so often, greatly strengthen-
ed many who were ready to faint ; and gave some
check to the designs of the papists to gain prose-
lytes. But God's time of deliverance was not
yet come ; as to some particular persons, their
temptations and trials were increased ; and some
abused, because they refused a compliance with
their superstitions. A young woman of our town
met with a new trial ; for on a day, a Frenchman
came into the room where she was, and shewed
her his beads, and boasted of them, putting them
near to her ; she knocked them out of his hands

on the floor ; for which fhe was beaten, and
threatened with death, and for fome days im-
prifoned. I pleaded with God his over-ruling
this firft effay for the deliverance of fome, as a
pledge of the reft being delivered in due time. I
implored captain de Beauville, who had always
been very friendly, to intercede with the governour for the return of my eldeft daughter; and
for his purchafing my fon Stephen from the
Indians at St. François fort ; and for liberty to
go up and fee my children and neighbours at
Montreal. Divine providence appeared to the
moderating my affliction, in that five Englifh
perfons of our town were permitted to return
with captain Livingfton, among whom went my
eldeft daughter. And my fon Stephen was redeemed, and fent to live with me : He was almoft quite naked, and very poor ; he had fuffered much among the Indians. One of the jefuits
took upon him to come to the wigwam and whip
him, on fome complaint that the fquaws had
made, that he did not work enough for them.
As to my petition for going up to Montreal to
fee my children and neighbours, it was denied ;
as my former defire of coming up to the city, before captain Livingfton's coming, was. God
granted me favour as to two of my petitions, but
yet brought me by his grace to be willing, that
he fhould glorify himfelf in difpofing of me and
mine as he pleafed, and knew to be moft for his
glory : And almoft always before any remarkable
favour, I was brought to lie down at the foot of
God, and made to be willing that God fhould
govern the world fo as might be moft for his own
honour,

honour, and brought to refign all to his holy
fovereignty : A frame of fpirit, when wrought in
me by the grace of God, giving the greateft con-
tent and fatisfaction ; and very often a fore-run-
ner of the mercy afked of God, or a plain de-
monftration, that the not obtaining my requeft
was beft for me. I had no fmall refrefhing, in
having one of my children with me for four
months. And the Englifh were, many of them,
ftrengthened with hopes, that the treaty betwixt
the governments would iffue in opening a door of
efcape for all.

In Auguft Mr. Dudley and captain Vetch arrived, and great encouragements were given as to
an exchange of all in the fpring of the year :
And fome few again were fent home ; among
whom I obtained leave to fend my fon Stephen.

Upon Mr. Dudley's and captain Vetch's pe-
titioning, I was again permitted to go up to
Quebec ; but difputing with a mendicant friar,
who faid, he was an Englifhman fent from France,
to endeavour the converfion of the Englifh at
Quebec, who arrived at Canada whilft our gentlemen were there, I was, by the priefts' means,
ordered to return again to Chateauviche, and no
other reafon given, but becaufe I difcourfed with
that prieft, and their fear I fhould prevent his fuccefs amongft the captives. But God fhewed his
diflike of fuch a perfecuting fpirit ; for the very
next day, which was September 20, O. S. October 1, N. S. the feminary, a very famous build-
ing, was moft of it burnt down, occafioned by a
joiner's letting a coal of fire drop among the
fhavings. The chapel in the prieft's garden, and
the

the great crofs, were burnt down ; the library of
the priefts burnt up.   This feminary and another
library had been burnt but about three years before.   The day after my being fent away, by the
priefts' means, from Quebec, at firft, there was
a thunder-ftorm, and the lightning ftruck the
feminary in the very place where the fire now
began.

A little before Mr. Dudley's arrival, came a
foldier into my landlord's houfe, barefoot and
barelegged, going on a pilgrimage to Saint Anne :
For, faid he, my captain, who died fome years
ago, appeared to me, and told me he was in-
purgatory ; and told me I muft go a pilgrimage
to Saint Anne, doing penance, and get a mafs
faid for him, and then he fhould be delivered.
Many believed him, and were much affected with
it ; came and told me of it, to gain my credit of
their devifed purgatory.   The foldier told me,
the priefts had counfelled him to undertake this
pilgrimage.   And, I am apt to think, ordered
his calling in at my landlord's, that I might fee
and fpeak with him.   I laughed at the conceit,
that a foldier muft be pitched upon to be fent
on this errand ; but they were much difpleafed,
and lamented my obftinacy, in that I would not
be reclaimed from a denial of purgatory by fuch a
miraculous providence.

As I was able, I fpread the cafe before God,
befeeching of him to difappoint them of their
expectations to profelyte any of the captives by
this ftratagem ; and by the goodnefs of God, it
was not very ferviceable ; for the foldier's converfation was fuch, that feveral among the French
themfelves.

themfelves judged it to be a forgery. And though the captain, fpoken of, was the governour's lady's brother, I never more heard any concernment or care to get him out of purgatory.

One of the parifh, where I lived, told me, that on the twenty-fecond of July, 1705, he was at Quebec, at the mendicant friar's church, on one of their feaft days, in honour of a great faint of their order, and that at five o'clock mafs, in the morning, near two hundred perfons being prefent, a great grey cat brake or pufhed afide fome glafs, entered into the church, paffed along near the altar, and put out five or fix candles, which were burning ; and that no one could tell which way the cat went out ; and he thought it was the devil.

When I was in the city in September, I faw two Englifh maids, who had lived with the Indians a long time. They told me, that an Indian had died at the place where they were ; and that when fundry of his relations were together, in order to attend his burial, the dead arofe, and informed them, " That at his death he went to hell, and there he faw all the Indians that had been dead fince their embracing the popifh religion ; and warned them to leave it off, or they would be damned too ;" and laid down dead again. They faid, the Indians were frightened, and very melancholy ; but the jefuit, to whom they told this, told them it was only a delufion of the devil, to draw them away from the true religion ; adding, that he knew for certain that all thofe Indians who had been dead, fpoken of by that Indian, were in heaven ; only one fquaw was gone to

E 2                                                          hell,

hell, who died without baptifm. Thefe maids faid alfo, that many of the Indians much lamented their making a war againft the Englifh, at the inftigation of the French.

The priefts, after Mr. Dudley's going from Canada, were ready to think their time was fhort for gaining Englifh profelytes, and doubled their diligence and wiles to gain over perfons to their perfuafion. I improved all opportunities I could, to write to the Englifh, that in that way I might be ferviceable to them. But many or moft of my letters, treating about religion, were intercepted, and burnt. I had a letter fent down to me by order of the governour, that I had liberty of writing to my children and friends, which fhould be continued, provided I wrote about indifferent things, and faid nothing in them about the points in controverfy between them and us : And if I were fo hardy as to write letters otherwife, they fhould endeavour to prevent their being delivered. Accordingly, I found many of them were burnt. But fometimes notice would be given to the Englifh, that there were letters written, but that they were burnt ; fo that their writing was fome-what ufeful, though never perufed by the Englifh, becaufe they judged thofe letters condemned popery. Many of our letters, written from New-England, were never delivered, becaufe of fome expreffions about religion in them. And, as I faid before, after Mr. Dudley's departure from Quebec, endeavours were very vigorous to feduce. Some were flattered with large promifes, others were threatened, and beaten, becaufe they would not turn. And when two Englifh women, who

had

had always oppofed their religion, were fick in the hofpital, they kept with them night and day, till they died ; and their friends kept from coming to vifit them. After their death, they gave out, that they died in the Romifh faith, and were received into their communion. Before their death, maffes were faid for them ; and they were buried in the church yard, with all their ceremonies. And after this, letters were fent into all parts, to inform the Englifh, that thefe two women turned to their religion before their death ; and that it concerned them to follow their example, for they could not be more obftinate than thofe women were, in their health, againft the Romifh faith, and yet on a death bed embraced it. They told the Englifh who lived near, that our religion was a dangerous religion to die in. But I fhall hereafter relate the juft grounds we have to think thefe things were falfehoods.

I was informed, there was an Englifh girl bid to take and wear the crofs, and crofs herfelf : She refufed ; they threatened her, and fhewed her the crofs. At length, fhe had her choice, either to crofs herfelf, and take the crofs, or be whipt, fhe chofe to be whipt ; and they made as though they would correct her ; but feeing her choofing indeed to fuffer rather than comply, they defifted, and tied the crofs about her neck. Some were taken and fhut up among their religious, and all forts of means ufed to gain them.

I received a letter from one of my neighbours, wherein he thus bewails : ‘ I obtained leave of my mafter to go to the Macqua fort, to fee my children, that I had not feen for a long time.
‘ I carried

'I carried a letter from my mafter, to fhew that I
'had leave to come.  When I came to the fort,
'I heard one of my children was in the woods.  I
'went to fee a boy I had there, who lived with
'one of the jefuits ; I had juft afked him of his
'welfare ; he faid his mafter would come prefent-
'ly ; he durft not ftay to fpeak with me now,
'being in fuch awe of his mafter.  On which I
'withdrew ; and when his mafter came in, I went
'and afked leave of him to fpeak with my child,
'and fhewed him my letter.  But he abfolutely
'refufed to let me fee or fpeak with him ; and
'faid, I had brought no letter from the govern-
'our, and would not permit me to ftay in the fort,
'though I had travelled on foot near fifty miles,
'for no other errand than to fee and fpeak with
'my children.'

The fame perfon, with another Englifhman,
laft fpring, obtained leave of the governour general to go to the fame fort on the fame errand, and
carried letters from the governour to the jefuits,
that he might be permitted to fpeak with his
children.  The letter was delivered to the jefuits ;
who told him, his fon was not at home, but gone
a hunting : Whereas he was hid from them, as he
heard afterward ; fo the poor man loft his labour
a fecond time.  Thefe men fay, that when they
returned to Montreal, one Laland, who was appointed as a fpy, always to obferve the motions of
the Englifh, told them, that one of the jefuits
had come in before them, and had told the governour that the lad was gone out a hunting : And
that the Englifhman, who accompanied this poor
man, went out into the woods, in hopes of finding
the

the lad ; and faw him, but the lad run away ; and that he followed him, and called after him, but he would not ftop ; but holding out a gun, threatened to fhoot him down, if he followed him ; and fo he was difcouraged, and turned back. And, fays Laland, you will never leave going to fee your children and neighbours, till fome of you are killed. But the men told him, it was an abfolute lie, let who would report it ; for they had neither feen the lad, nor did they go into the woods to fearch after him. They judge this was told to the governour, to prevent any Englifh for the future going to fee their children and neighbours. Some of ours fay, they have been little better than abfolutely promifed to have their children, who are among the favages, in cafe they themfelves would embrace popery. And that the priefts had faid, they had rather the children fhould be among the Indians, as they were, than be brought out by the French, and fo. be in readinefs to return for New-England.

A maid of our town was put into a religious houfe, among the nuns, for more than two years, and all forts of means, by flatteries, threatenings, and abufive carriages, ufed to bring her to turn. They offered her money, which when refufed, efpecially the latter part of the time, they threatened her very much ; fent for her before them, and commanded her to crofs herfelf. She refufed, they hit her a box on the ear ; bid her again, ftill fhe refufed. They ordered a rod with fix branches full of knots to be brought ; and when fhe refufed, they ftruck her on the hands, ftill renewing their commands ; and fhe ftood to her
refufals,

refufals, till her hands were filled with wales, with the blows. But one faid, Beat her no more, we will give her to the Indians, if fhe will not turn. They pinched her arms till they were black and blue ; and made her go into their church ; and becaufe fhe would not crofs herfelf, ftruck her feveral blows with their hands on her face. A fquaw was brought in, and faid, fhe was fent to fetch her to the Indians ; but fhe refufed ; the fquaw went away, and faid, fhe would bring her hufband with her to-morrow, and fhe fhould be carried away by force. She told me, fhe remembered what I told her one day, after the nuns had threatened to give her away to the Indians ; that they only faid fo to affright her, that they never would give her away. The nuns told her, fhe fhould not be permitted any more to fpeak to the Englifh ; and that they would afflict her without giving her any reft, if fhe refufed : But God preferved her from falling. This poor girl had many prayers going up to Heaven for her daily, and by name, becaufe her trials were more known to fome of the Englifh, than the trials of others, who lived more remote from them.

Here might be a hiftory by itfelf, of the trials and fufferings of many of our children, and young ones, who have been abufed, and after feparation from grown perfons, made to do as they would have them.

I fhall here give an account of what was done to one of my children, a boy between fifteen and fixteen years of age, two hundred miles diftant from me, which occafioned grief and forrow, that I want words to utter ; and yet kept under fuch

awe,

awe, that he never durft write any thing to me,
for fear of being difcovered in writing about religion.   They threatened to put him to the Indians again, if he would not turn ; telling him,
he was never bought out of their hands, but only
fojourned with them, but if he would turn, he
fhould never be put into their hands any more.
The priefts would fpend whole days in urging
him.   He was fent to fchool to learn to read and
write French ; the fchool-mafter fometimes flattered him with promifes, if he would crofs himfelf ; then threatened him if he would not.   But
when he faw flattering promifes of rewards, and
threatenings, were ineffectual, he ftruck him with
a ftick he had in his hand ; and when he faw
that would not do, he made him get down on his
knees about an hour ; and then came and bid
him make the fign of the crofs, and that without
any delay ; he ftill refufed.   Then he gave him
a couple of ftrokes, with a whip he had in his
hand ; which whip had three branches, and
about twelve great knots tied in it.   And again
bid him make the fign of the crofs ; and if it
was any fin, he would bear it himfelf : And faid
alfo, You are afraid you fhall be changed if you
do it : But (faid he) you will be the fame, your
fingers will not be changed.   And after he had
made him fhed many tears, under his abufes and
threatenings, he told him, he would have it done :
And fo through cowardice and fear of the whip,
he made the fign.   And did fo for feveral days
together, with much ado, he was brought to crofs
himfelf.   And then the mafter told him, he
would have it done without his particular bidding
him.

him. And when he came to fay his leffon, and
croffed not himfelf, the mafter faid, have you forgot what I bid you do ? No, fir, faid he ; then
the fchoolmafter faid, Down on your knees ; and
fo kept him for an hour and half, till fchool was
done ; and fo did for about a week. When he
faw this would not do, he took the whip, What,
will not you do it, (faid he), I will make you :
And fo again frighted him to a compliance.
After this, he commanded him to go to the
church : When he refufed, he told him, he would
make him. And one morning fent four of the
biggeft boys of the fchool, to draw him by force
to mafs. Thefe, with other feverities and witty
ftratagems, were ufed ; and I utterly ignorant of
any attempt made upon him, to bring him to
change his religion. His fear was fuch, that he
never durft write any of thefe things, left his letters fhould fall into their hands, and he fhould
again be delivered to the Indians. Hearing of
an opportunity of writing to him by one of the
parifh where I was, going up to Montreal, I
wrote a letter to him, and had by him a letter
from my fon ; which I fhall here infert.

   " *Honoured Father,*

   " I HAVE received your letter, bearing date
January 11, 1705,6 ; for which I give you many
thanks, with my duty and my brother's. I am
forry you have not received all the letters I have
written to you ; as I have not received all yours.
According to your good counfel, I do almoft
every day read fomething of the bible, and fo
ftrengthen my faith. As to the captives newly
brought, Lancafter is the place of two of them,
                                                    and

and Marlborough that of the third ; the governour of Montreal has them all three. There is
other news that will feem more ftrange to you :
That two Englifh women, who in their life time
were dreadfully fet againft the catholick religion,
did on their death bed embrace it. The one
Abigail Turbet, the other of them Efther Jones,
both of them known to you. Abigail Turbet
fent for Mr. Meriel the Sabbath before fhe died ;
and faid (many a time upon feveral following
days) that fhe committed her foul into his hands,
and was ready to do whatever he pleafed. She
defired him to go to the chapel St. Anne, and
there to fay a holy mafs for her, that fhe might
have her fins pardoned, and the will of the Lord
accomplifhed upon her. Her coufin, Mrs. Bad-
fton, now Stilfon, afked her, whether fhe fhould
be willing to do as fhe faid ; fhe anfwered, yes.
And upon the Tuefday fhe was taken into the
catholick church, in the prefence of John Laland,
and madam Grizalem, an Englifh woman, and
Mrs. Stilfon, alfo with many French people befides. She was anointed with oil on the fame
day, according to her will then. Upon the
Wednefday following, an image of Chrift crucifi-
ed was brought to her ; fhe caufed it to be fet
up over againft her, at the curtains of her bed,
and looked continually upon the fame ; and alfo
a little crucifix was brought unto her ; fhe took it,
and kiffed it, and laid it upon her ftomach. She
did alfo make the fign of the crofs upon herfelf,
when fhe took any meat or drink. She promifed to God, that if fhe fhould recover, fhe would
go to the mafs every day : She having on her

F                                            hand

hand a crucifix, said, Oh, my Lord, that I should
have known thee so late ! She did also make a
prayer to the Virgin Mary, the two last days of
the week.   She could utter no word, but by kis-
sing the crucifix, and endeavouring to cross her-
self, she gave an evidence of her faith.   She died
on Saturday the 24th of November, at three
o'clock in the afternoon.   The next day, the
priest did commend that woman's soul to the
prayers of the congregation in the mass ; in the
afternoon she was honourably buried in the
church yard, next to the church, close to the
body of the justice Pese's wife ; all the people
being present at her funeral.   The same day, in
the evening, Mr. Meriel, with an English woman, went to Esther Jones ; she did at first disdain ; but a little after, she confessed there were
seven sacraments, Christ's body present, the sacrament of the mass, the inequality of power among
the pastors of the church ; and being returned to
wait by her all night long, he read and expound-
ed to her some part of the catholick confession of
faith to her satisfaction.   About midnight he
asked her, whether she might not confess her
sins ; I doubt not but I may, said she : And two
hours after, she made unto him a fervent confession of all the sins of her whole life : When he
said, he was to offer Christ to his father for her,
she liked it very well.   The superior of the nuns
being come in to see her, she now desired that
she might receive Christ's body before she died.
She did also show Mrs. Stilson a great mind to
receive the sacrament of extreme unction, and
said, that if ever she should recover and get home,
                                             she

fhe would reproach the minifters for their neg-
lecting that facrament, fo plainly commanded
by St. James. In the afternoon, after fhe had
begged pardon for her wavering, and the catholick confeffion of faith was read aloud to her, in
the hearing of Mr. Crafton, Mrs. Stilfon, and
another Englifh woman, fhe owned the fame.
About feven o'clock the fame day, fhe faid to
Mr. Dubifon, fhall not they give me the holy
communion ? But her tongue was then fo thick
that fhe could hardly fwallow any thing. She
was then anointed with holy oil : But before, fhe
faid to Mr. Meriel, why have you not yet, fir, for-
given my fins ? In the night following, that prieft,
and Mr. Dubifon, were continually by her ; and
fometimes praying to God in her name, and praying to the Virgin Mary, and other faints. She
faid alfo, I believe all : I am very glad Chrift
was offered to his Father for me. Six or feven
hours before fhe died, a crucifix was fhowed to
her by Mr. Dubifon ; fhe took it, and laid it
upon her heart, and kiffed it ; and then the nuns
hanged it with a pair of beads upon her neck.
A little before fhe died, Mr. Dubifon afked her
to pray for him in heaven ; fhe promifed him :
So fhe gave up the ghoft, at ten of the clock, the
27th of November, whilft the high mafs was
faying ; fhe was foon commended to the prayers.
On the fourth day of the week following fhe was
buried, after the mafs had been faid for her. She
was laid by Abigail Turbet. Jan. 23, 1705,6.''

I HAVE here tranfcribed the letter in the
very words of it, without the leaft alteration :
The

The fame for fubftance was fent to feveral other captives. When I had this letter, I prefently knew it to be of Mr. Meriel's compofing : But the meffenger, who brought the letter, brought word that my fon had embraced their religion. Afterwards, when fome blamed him for letting me know of it, becaufe (they faid) they feared my forrow would fhorten my days ; he told me, he thought with himfelf, that if he was in my cafe he fhould be willing to know the worft, and therefore told me, as he would have defired to have known if in my place. I thanked him, acknowledging it a favour to let me know of it ; but the news was ready to overwhelm me with grief and forrow. I made my complaint to God, and mourned before him ; forrow and anguifh took hold upon me. I afked of God to direct me what to do, and how to write, and find out an opportunity of conveying a letter to him ; and committed this difficulty to his providence. I now found a greater oppofition to a patient, quiet, humble refignation to the will of God than I fhould otherwife have known, if not fo tried. Here I thought of my afflictions and trials ; my wife and two children killed, and many of my neighbours ; and myfelf, fo many of my children and friends in a popifh captivity, feparated from our children, not capable to come to them to inftruct them in the way they ought to go ; and cunning, crafty enemies, ufing all their fubtilty to infinuate into young ones, fuch principles as would be pernicious. I thought with myfelf how happy many others were, in that they had their children with them, under all advantages to

bring

bring them up in the nurture and admonition of
the Lord ; whilft we were feparated one from
another, and our children in great peril of embracing damnable doctrines.   Oh ! that all parents, who read this hiftory, would blefs God for
the advantages they have of educating their
children, and faithfully improve it ! I mourned
when I thought with myfelf that I had one child
with the Macquas, a fecond turned to popery,
and a little child, of fix years of age, in danger
from a child to be inftructed in popery ; and
knew full well that all endeavours would be ufed
to prevent my feeing or fpeaking with them.
But in the midft of all thefe, God gave me a fecret hope, that he would magnify his power and
free grace, and difappoint all their crafty defigns.
When I looked on the right hand and on the
left, all refuge failed me, and none fhewed any
care for my foul.   But God brought that word
to uphold me ; *Who is able to do exceeding abun-*
*dantly above what we can afk or think.*   As alfo
that, *Is any thing too hard for God ?* I prayed to
God to direct me ; and wrote very fhort the firft
time, and in general terms, fearing left if I fhould
write about things in controverfy, my letters
would not come to him.   I therefore addreffed
him with the following letter.

" *Son Samuel,*

" YOURS of January 23, I received, and with
it had the tidings that you had made an abjuration
of the Proteftant faith for the Romifh : News
that I heard with the moft diftreffing, afflicting,
forrowful fpirit that ever I heard any news.  Oh !
I pity you, I mourn over you day and night !

Oh ! I pity your weaknefs, that through the craftinefs of man you are turned from the fimplicity of the gofpel ! I perfuade myfelf you have done it through ignorance. Oh ! why have you neglected to afk a father's advice in an affair of fo great importance as the change of religion ! God knows that the catechifm, in which I inftructed you, is according to the word of God ; and fo will be found in the day of judgment. Oh ! confider and bethink yourfelf what you have done ! And whether you afk me or not, my poor child, I cannot but pray for you, that you may be recovered out of the fnare you are taken in. Read the bible, pray in fecret ; make Chrift's righteoufnefs your only plea before God, for juftification : Beware of all immorality, and of profaning God's Sabbaths. Let a father's advice be afked for the future, in all things of weight and moment. What is a man profited if he gain the whole world, and lofe his own foul ? Or what fhall a man give in exchange for his foul ? I defire to be humbled under the mighty hand of God thus afflicting of me. I would not do as you have done for ten thoufand worlds. My heart aches within me, but I will yet wait upon the Lord ; to him will I commit your cafe day and night : He can perform all things for me and mine ; and can yet again recover you from your fall. He is a God forgiving iniquity, tranfgreffion and fin : To the Lord our God belong forgiveneffes, though we have rebelled. I charge you not to be inftrumental to enfnare your poor brother Warham, or any other, and fo add fin to fin. Accept of my love, and do not forfake a
father's

father's advice, who above all things defires that your foul may be faved in the day of the Lord."

WHAT I mournfully wrote, I followed with my poor cries to God in heaven to make effectu-al, to caufe in him a confideration of what he had done. God faw what a proud heart I had, and what need I had to be fo anfwered out of the whirlwind, that I might be humbled before him. Not having any anfwer to my letter for fome weeks, I wrote the following letter, as I was enabled of God, and fent to him by a faithful hand ; which, by the blefling of God, was made effectual for his good, and the good of others, who had fallen to popery ; and for the eftablifh-ing and ftrengthening of others to refift the effays of the adverfary to truth. God brought good out of this evil, and made what was defigned to pro-mote their intereft, an occafion of fhame to them.

" *Son Samuel*,

" I HAVE waited till now for an anfwer from you, hoping to hear from you, why you made an abjuration of the Proteftant faith for the Romifh. But fince you continue to neglect to write to me about it, as you neglected to take any advice or counfel from a father, when you did it, I cannot forbear writing again, and making fome reflec-tions on the letter you wrote me laft, about the two women. It feems to me, from thofe words of Abigail Turbet's, in your letter, or rather of Mr. Meriel's, which you tranfcribed for him— [Abigail Turbet fent for Mr. Meriel, committed her foul into his hand, and was ready to do what-foever he pleafed]—I fay, it feems rational to
believe

believe, that she had not the use of her reason ; it is an expression to be abhorred by all who have any true sense of religion.    Was Mr. Meriel a God, a Christ ?  Could he bear to hear such words and not reject them ; replying, " do not commit your soul into my hands, but see that you commit your soul into the hands of God through Christ Jesus, and do whatever God commands you in his holy word.    As for me, I am a creature, and cannot save your soul ; but will tell you of Acts iv. 12. *Neither is there salvation in any other ; for there is no other name under heaven given among men, whereby we must be saved.*"    Had he been a faithful minister of Jesus Christ, he would have said, " It is an honour due to Christ alone. The holy apostle says, *Now unto him that is able to keep you, and present you faultless before the presence of his glory, with exceeding joy, to the only wise God our Saviour, be glory, and majesty, dominion and power, both now and ever, amen.*"    Jude, 24, 25, verses.    As to what you write about praying to the Virgin Mary, and other saints, I make this reply, Had Mr. Meriel done his duty, he would have said to them, as 1 John, ii. 1, 2. *If any man sin, we have an advocate with the Father, Jesus Christ the righteous ; and he is the propitiation for our sins.*    The scriptures say, *There is one God, and one mediator between God and man, the man Christ Jesus.*    Yea, Christ said, go and preach, *He that believeth and is baptized, shall be saved.*    The apostle, in Gal. i. 8. saith, *But though we or an angel from heaven preach any other gospel unto you, than that we have preached to you, let him be accursed.* They never preached, that we should pray to the

Virgin

Virgin Mary, or other faints.   As you would be
faved, hear what the apostle faith, Heb. iv.
13, &c.  *Neither is there any creature that is not
manifest in his fight ; but all things are naked, and
open unto the eyes of him with whom we have to
do.   Seeing then that we have a great high priest that
is entered into the heavens, Jefus the fon of God, let
us hold faft our profeffion : For we have not an high
priest that cannot be touched with the feelings of our
infirmities, but was in all points tempted like as we
are, yet without fin ; let us therefore come boldly unto
the throne of grace, that we may obtain mercy, and find
grace to help in time of need.*   Which words do
hold forth, how that Chrift Jefus is in every
refpect qualified to be a mediator and interceffor ;
and I am fure they cannot be applied to any mere
creature, to make them capable of our religious
truft.   When Roman catholicks have faid all
they can, they are not able to prove, that the
faints in heaven have a knowledge of what prayers,
are directed to them.   Some fay they know then
one way, others fay they have the knowledge of
them in another way : And that which they have
fixed upon as moft probable to them, is, that
they know of them from their beholding the face
of God ; feeing God, they know thefe prayers :
But this is a great miftake.   Though the faints
fee and know God in a glorious manner, yet they
have not an infinite knowledge ; and it does no
ways follow, that becaufe they fee God, they
know all prayers that are directed to them upon
the earth.   And God has no where in his word
told us, that the faints have fuch a knowledge.
Befides, were it a thing poffible for them to have
a knowledge

a knowledge of what prayers are directed to them, it does not follow that they are to be prayed to, or have religious honour conferred upon them. The Romanists can neither give one scripture precept or example for praying to them ; but God has provided a mediator, who knows all our petitions, and is faithful and merciful enough ; and we have both scripture precept and example, to look to him as our mediator and advocate with the Father. Further, it cannot be proved that it is consistent with the saints being creatures, as well as with their happiness, to have a knowledge of prayers from all parts of the world at the same time, from many millions together, about things so vastly differing one from another : And then to present those supplications for all that look to them, is not humility, but will-worship. Col. ii. 18. *Let no man beguile you of your reward, in a voluntary humility, worshipping of angels,* verse 23. *Which things indeed have a shew of wisdom and will-worship, and humility.* For what humility can it be, to distrust the way that God has provided and encouraged us to come to him in, and impose upon God a way of our own devising ? Was not God angry with Jeroboam for imposing upon him after such a sort ? 1 Kings, xii. 33. *So he offered upon the altar which he had made in Bethel, the fifth day of the eighth month, which he devised of his own heart.* Therefore Christ saith, Mark vii. 7. *Howbeit, in vain do they worship me, teaching for doctrines the commandments of men.* Before the coming of Christ, and his entering into heaven as an intercessor ; Heb. vii. 25. *Wherefore he is able to save them to the uttermost*
that

*that come to God by him, seeing he ever liveth to make*
*interceſſion for them ;* I ſay, before Chriſt's entering into heaven as an interceſſor, there is not
one word of any prayer to ſaints ; and what reaſon can be given that now there is need of ſo
many ſaints to make interceſſion, when Chriſt as
a prieſt is entered into heaven to make intercef-
ſion for us ? The anſwer that the Romaniſts give
is a very fable and falſehood : Namely, that there
were no ſaints in heaven till after the reſurrection
and aſcenſion of Chriſt, but were reſerved in a
place called Limbus Patrum, and ſo had not the
beatifical viſion. See Gen. v. 24. *Enoch walked*
*with God, and was not, for God took him.* If he
was not taken into heaven, what can be the ſenſe
of thoſe words, *for God took him ?* Again, 2 Kings,
ii. 1. When the Lord would take up Elijah into
heaven by a whirlwind, verſe 11. *There appeared*
*a chariot of fire and horſes of fire, and parted them*
*both aſunder, and Elijah went up by a whirlwind*
*into heaven.* Muſt the truth of the ſcripture be
called in queſtion to uphold their notions ? Beſides, it is not conſiſtent with reaſon to ſuppoſe,
that Enoch and Elias, inſtead of having a peculiar privilege vouchſafed to them, for their em-
inency in holineſs, ſhould be leſs happy for ſo
long a time than the reſt of the ſaints deceaſed,
who are glorified in heaven ; which muſt be, if
they are yet kept, and muſt be, till the day of
judgment out of heaven, and the beatifical viſion,
in an earthly paradiſe, according to ſome of the
Romaniſts ; or in ſome other place, they know
not where, according to others. Religious wor-
ſhip is not to be given to the creature, Mat. iv.
9, 10,

9, 10, and faith, *All thefe things will I give thee, if thou wilt fall down and worfhip me.* Then faith Jefus to him, *Get thee hence, Satan ; for it is written, thou fhalt worfhip the Lord thy God, and him only fhalt thou ferve.* That phrafe, *and him only fhalt thou ferve,* excludes all creatures. Rev. xxii. 8, 9. *I fell down to worfhip before the feet of the angel, which fhewed me thefe things ; then faith he to me, fee thou do it not, for I am thy fellow fervant, and of thy brethren the prophets, and of them which keep the fayings of this book, worfhip God.* Which plainly fhews, that God only is to be worfhipped with a religious worfhip. None can think that Saint John intended to give the higheft divine worfhip to the angel, who faith, *Do not fall down and worfhip me ; it is God's due, worfhip God.* So Acts x. 25, 26. *As Peter was coming in, Cornelius met him and fell down at his feet, and worfhipped him ; but Peter took him up, faying, ftand up, I myfelf alfo am a man.* See alfo Lev. xix. 10. The words of the fecond commandment (which the Romanifts either leave out, or add to the firft commandment, faying, *Thou fhalt have no other gods before me,* adding, &c.) I fay the words of the fecond commandment are, *Thou fhalt not make to thyfelf any graven image, or any likenefs of any thing that is in heaven above, or that is in the earth beneath, or that is in the waters under the earth ; thou fhalt not bow down thyfelf to them nor ferve them, for I the Lord thy God am a jealous God,* &c. Thefe words being inferted in the letter which came from your brother Eleazer, in New-England, the laft fummer, was the caufe of the letters being fent down from Montreal, and not given to you,
when

when fo near you, as I fuppofe, there being no
other claufe of the letter that could be objected againft, and the reafon why found at Quebec,
when I fent it to you a fecond time, enclofed in
a letter written by myfelf.    The brazen ferpent,
made by divine appointment as a type of Chrift,
when abufed to fuperftition, was by reforming
Hezekiah broken in pieces.    As to what the
Romanifts plead about the lawfulnefs of image
and faint worfhip, from thofe likeneffes of things
made in Solomon's temple, it is nothing to the
purpofe.    We do not fay it is not lawful to make
or have a picture ; but thofe carved images were
not, in the temple, to be adored, bowed down to,
or worfhipped.    There is no manner of confe-
quence, that becaufe there were images made in
Solomon's temple that were not adored and worfhipped, that therefore it is now lawful to make
and fall down before images, and pray to them,
and fo worfhip them.

" Religious worfhipping of faints cannot be
defended from, but is forbidden, in the fcriptures ;
and for fear of lofing their difciples, the Romanifts keep away from them the bible, and oblige
them to believe as they fay they muft believe ;
as though there was no ufe to be made of our
reafon about our fouls ; and yet the Bereans were
counted noble for fearching the fcriptures, to fee
whether the things preached by Saint Paul were
fo or not.    They dare not allow you liberty to
fpeak with your father, or others, for fear their
errors fhould be difcovered to you.    Again, you
write, " that Efther Jones confeffed that there
was an inequality of power among the paftors of
G                                         the

the church." An argument to convince the world, that becaufe the priefts, in fallacious ways, caufed a woman, diftempered with a very high fever, if not diftracted, to fay, fhe confeffed there was an inequality of power among the paftors of the church, therefore all the world are obliged to believe that there is a pope. An argument to be fent from Dan to Beerfheba, every where, where any Englifh captives are, to gain their belief of a pope. Can any rational man think that Chrift, in the 16th chapter of Matthew, gave Saint Peter fuch a power as the papifts fpeak of ; or that the difciples fo underftood Chrift ? When immediately there arofe a difpute among them, who fhould be the greateft in the kingdom of heaven ? Matth. xviii. 1. *At the fame time came the difciples of Jefus, faying, who is the greateft in the kingdom of heaven ?* The rock fpoken of in the 16th of Matthew, not the perfon of Peter, but the confeffion made by him, and the fame power is given to all the difciples, if you compare one fcripture with another ; not one word in any place of fcripture of fuch a vicarfhip power as of a pope, nor any folid foundation of proof that Peter had a greater authority than the reft of the apoftles. 1 Cor. iv. 6. *That you might learn in us, not to think of men above that which is written.* Yea, the apoftle condemns them, 1 Cor. i. 12. for their contentions, *One faying, I am of Paul, I of Apollos, and I of Cæphas ,* no more of Peter's being a foundation than any of the reft. *For we are built upon the foundation of the apoftles and prophets, Jefus Chrift himfelf being the chief corner ftone.* Not one word in any of Peter's epiftles, fhowing

that

that he had greater power than the other apostles.
Nay, if the scriptures give any preference, it is to
Saint Paul rather than Saint Peter. 1 Cor. iii. 10.
*According to the grace of God which is given to me,*
*as a wise master builder I have laid the foundation.*
1 Cor. v. 3, 4. *For I verily as absent in body, but*
*present in spirit, have judged already, as though I*
*were present, concerning him that hath so done this*
*deed.* *In the name of our Lord Jesus Christ, when*
*ye are gathered together, and my spirit, with the pow-*
*er of our Lord Jesus Christ,* &c. 1 Cor. vii. 1.
*Now concerning the things whereof ye wrote to me ;*
application made not to Saint Peter, but Paul,
for the decision of a controversy or scruple.
1 Cor. xi. 2. *Now I praise you, brethren, that you*
*remember me in all things, and keep the ordinance as*
*I delivered them to you.* Either those spoken of,
Acts xv. or in his ministry and epistles, 2 Cor. ii.
10. *For your sake, forgave I it, in the person of*
*Christ.* 2 Cor. xi. 28. *That which cometh upon me*
*daily, the care of all the churches.* 2 Cor. xii. 11,
12. *For in nothing am I behind the very chiefest of the*
*apostles, though I be nothing.* *Truly the signs of an*
*apostle were wrought among you in all patience, in signs*
*and wonders, and mighty deeds ;* and in other places.
Again, if you consult Acts xv. where you have an
account of the first synod or council, you will
find that the counsel or sentence of the apostle
James is followed, verse 19. Wherefore my sentence is, &c. not a word that Saint Peter was
chief. Again, you find Peter himself sent forth
by the other apostles, Acts viii. 14. *The apostles*
*sent unto them, Peter and John.* When the
church of the Jews found fault with Peter, for
going

going in to the Gentiles when he went to Cornelius, he does not say, Why do you queſtion me,
or call me to an account, I am Chriſt's vicar on
earth.    When Paul reproved Peter, Gal. ii. he
does not defend himſelf, by mentioning an infal-
libility in himſelf as Chriſt's vicar, or reprove
Paul for his boldneſs.

" The Roman catholick church cannot be a
true church of Chriſt, in that it makes laws directly contrary to the laws and commands of
Chriſt :   As for example, in with-holding the
wine or the cup from the laity, in the Lord's
ſupper ;   whereas Chriſt commands the ſame to
drink who were to eat.   Their evaſion, that the
blood is in the body, and ſo they partake of both
in eating, is a great fallacy, built on a falſe foundation of tranſubſtantiation.   For when men eat,
they cannot be ſaid to drink, which Chriſt commands, for Chriſt commands that we *take the cup*
*and drink*, which is not done in eating ;   beſides,
the prieſts themſelves will not be ſo put off.
The words, *this is my body*, do only intend, *this*
*doth ſignify or repreſent my body*, which will appear
if you compare ſcripture with ſcripture ;   for after
the conſecration, the Holy Ghoſt calls it bread,
and the fruit of the vine.   Exod. xii. 11. *It is*
*the Lord's paſſover ;* that is, it repreſents it.   In
all the evangeliſts, you read of killing and eating
the paſſover, a few lines or verſes before theſe
words, *this is my body*, which plainly ſhow, that
our Saviour, in the ſame way of figurative expreſſion, ſpeaks of the goſpel ſacrament.   If theſe
words were taken as the Romaniſts expound them,
he muſt eat his own body himſelf, whole and entire

tire in his own hands ; and after that, each one
of the difciples eat him entire, and yet he fet at
the table whole, untouched, at the fame time ;
contradictions impoffible to be defended by any
rational arguments. Yea, his whole body muft
be now in heaven and in a thoufand other places,
and in the mouth of every communicant at the
fame time, and that both as a broken and un-
broken facrifice, and be fubject to putrefaction.
Chrift is faid to be a door, a true vine, a way, a
rock. What work fhall we make if we expound
thefe in a literal manner, as the Romanifts do,
when they fay, *this is my body*, means the real
body of Chrift in the eucharift ? It is faid, 1 Cor.
x. 4. *And did all drink the fame fpiritual drink :
For they drank of that fpiritual Rock that followed
them : And that rock was Chrift.* Was Chrift lit-
erally a rock, think you ? Yea, it is abfurd to
believe, that a prieft, uttering a few words over a
wafer not above an inch fquare, can make it a
God, or the body of Chrift entire, as it was offered
on the crofs. It is a blafphemy to pretend to a
power of making God at their pleafure ; and then
eat him, and give him to others to be eaten, or
fhut him up in their altars : That they can utter
the fame words, and make a God or not make a
God, according to their intention, and that the
people are obliged to believe that it is God, and
fo adore it, when they never hear any word of
confecration, nor know the prieft's intention.

" As to what you write about the holy mafs,
I reply, it is wholly an human invention ; not a
word of fuch a facrifice in the whole bible ; its
being a facrifice propitiatory daily to be offered,

is

is contrary to the holy fcriptures. Heb. vii. 27. *Who needeth not daily, as thofe high-priefts, to offer up facrifice firft for his own fins, and then for the people's : For this he did once, when he offered up himfelf.* And yet the Romanifts fay, there is need that he be offered up as a facrifice to God every day. Heb. ix. 12. *By his own blood he entered in once into the holy place, having obtained eternal redemption for us.* ver. 25, 26, 27, 28. *Nor yet that he fhould offer himfelf often, as the high-prieft entereth into the holy place, every year, with the blood of others : For then muft he often have fuffered fince the foundation of the world. But now once, in the end of the world, hath he appeared to put away fin by the facrifice of himfelf. As it is appointed unto men once to die, but after this the judgment ; fo Chrift was once offered to bear the fins of many.* Heb. x. 10. *By which will we are fanctified, through the offering of the body of Jefus Chrift once for all.* ver. 12. *But this man, after he had offered one facrifice for fins, forever fat down on the right-hand of God.* ver. 14. *For by one offering he hath perfected forever them that are fanctified.* By which fcriptures you may fee, that the mafs is not of divine appointment, but an human invention. Their evafion of a bloody and an unbloody facrifice, is a fham ; the holy fcriptures fpeak not one word of Chrift's being offered as a facrifice propitiatory, after fuch a fort as they call an unbloody facrifice. All the ceremonies of the mafs are human inventions, which God never commanded.

" As to what is in the letter about praying for the women after their death, it is very ridiculous. For as the tree falls, fo it lies ; as death leaves, judgment

judgment will find. No change after death from an afflicted to a happy place and ftate. Purgatory is a phantafm, for enriching the clergy, and impoverifhing the laity. The notion of it is a fatal fnare to many fouls, who fin with hopes of eafily getting prieftly abfolutions at death, and buying off torments with their money. The foul at death goes immediately to judgment, and fo to heaven or hell. No authentick place of fcripture mentions fo much as one word of any fuch place or ftate. Mr. Meriel told me, " If I found one error in our religion, it was enough to caufe me to difown our whole religion." By his argument, you may fee what reafon you have to avoid that religion that is fo full of errors. Bethink yourfelf, and confult the fcriptures, if you can get them : (I mean the bible). Can you think their religion is right, when they are afraid to let you have an Englifh bible ? Or to fpeak with your father, or other of your chriftian neighbours, for fear they fhould give you fuch convictions of truth that they cannot remove ? Can that religion be true, that cannot bear an examination from the fcriptures, which are a perfect rule in matters of faith ? Or that muft be upheld by ignorance, efpecially ignorance of the holy fcriptures ?

" Thefe things have I written, as in my heart I believe. I long for your recovery, and will not ceafe to pray for it. I am now a man of a forrowful fpirit, and look upon your fall as the moft aggravating circumftance of my afflictions, and am perfuaded that no pains will be wanting to prevent me from feeing or fpeaking with you ; but I know that God's grace is all-fufficient.

He

He is able to do exceeding abundantly above
what I can aſk or think.  Do not give way to
diſcouragement as to a return to New-England ;
read over what I have written, and keep it with
you if you can ; you have no friend on earth that
wiſheth your eternal ſalvation more heartily than
your father.  I long to ſee and ſpeak with you,
but I never forget you ; my love to you, and to
your brother and ſiſter, and to all our fellow-
priſoners.  Let me hear from you as often as you
can.  I hope God will appear for us before it be
long.

" There are a great many other things in the
letter, which deſerve to be refuted ; but I ſhall be
too tedious in remarking on them all at once :
Yet would not paſs over that paſſage in the letter
in which Eſther Jones confeſſed that there were
ſeven ſacraments.  To which I anſwer, That
ſome of the moſt learned of the Romiſh religion
confeſſed, (without the diſtracting pains of a violent fever), and left it upon record in print, that
it cannot be convincingly made out from the
ſcripture, that there are ſeven ſacraments, and
that their moſt inconteſtable proof is from tradition, and by their traditions they might have
found ſeventeen as well as ſeven ; conſidering
that four popes, ſucceſſively, ſpent their lives in
purging and correcting old authors.  But no man
can, out of the holy ſcriptures, prove any more
than two ſacraments of divine inſtitution, under
the New-Teſtament, namely, baptiſm and the
Lord's ſupper.  If you make the ſcriptures a
perfect rule of faith, as you ought to do, you cannot believe as the Romiſh church believers.  Oh !

ſee

fee that you fanctify the Lord himfelf in your heart, and make him your fear and your dread. Fear not them that can kill the body, and after that have no more that they can do ; but rather fear him that has power to deftroy foul and body in hell fire. The Lord have mercy upon you, and fhew you mercy, for the worthinefs and righteoufnefs fake of Jefus Chrift, our great and glorious Redeemer and Advocate, who makes in-terceffion for tranfgreffors. My prayers are daily offered to God for you, for your brother and fif-ter, yea for all my children, and fellow prifoners.

" I am your afflicted and forrowful father,

" JOHN WILLIAMS.

" Chateauviche, March 22, 1706."

GOD, who is glorioufly free and rich in his grace to vile finners, was pleafed to blefs poor and weak means for the recovery of my child fo taken, and gave me to fee, that he did not fay to the houfe of Jacob, Seek you me in vain. Oh ! that every reader would in ever difficulty make him their refuge ; he is a hopeful ftay. To alle-viate my forrow, I received the following letter in anfwer to mine.

*Montreal, May* 12, 1706.

" *Honoured Father,*

" I RECEIVED your letter which you fent by ———, which good letter I thank you for ; and for the good counfel which you gave me : I de-fire to be thankful for it, and hope it will be for the good of my foul. I may fay as in the pfalms ; *The forrows of death compaffed me, and the pains of hell gat hold on me: I found trouble and forrow, then called I upon the name of the Lord : O Lord, I be-feech*

*feech thee, deliver my foul! Gracious is the Lord and righteous, yea our God is merciful.* As for what you afk me about my making an abjuration of the proteftant faith for the Romifh, I durft not write fo plain to you as I would, but hope to fee and difcourfe with you. I am forry for the fin I have committed in changing of religion, for which I am greatly to blame. You may know that Mr. Meriel, the fchool-mafter, and others, were continually at me about it ; at laft I gave over to it ; for which I am very forry. As for that letter you had from me, it was a letter I tranfcribed for Mr. Meriel : And for what he faith about Abigail Turbet, and Efther Jones, no body heard them but he, as I underftand. I defire your prayes to God for me, to deliver me from my fins. Oh remember me in your prayers ! I am your dutiful fon, ready to take your counfel.

" SAMUEL WILLIAMS."

THIS prieft, Mr. Meriel, has brought many letters to him, and bid him write them over and fend them, and fo he has done for many others. By this, as alfo by Mrs. Stilfon's faying, " She does not think that either of thefe women did change their religion before their death ;" and alfo, " oftentimes during their ficknefs, whilft they had the ufe of their reafon, they protefted againft the Romifh religion and faith," it is evident that thefe women never died papifts, but that it was a wily ftratagem of the priefts to advance their religion : For letters were fent immediately, after their death, to ufe this as a perfuafive argument to gain others. But God in his providence

providence gave farther conviction of their fal-
lacioufnefs in this matter.

For the laft fummer, one Biggilow, of Marlborough, a captive at Montreal, was very fick in
the hofpital, and, in the judgment of all, with a
ficknefs to death. Then the priefts and others
gave out, that he was turned to be of their religion,
and taken into their communion : But, contrary to
their expectation, he was brought back from the
gates of death, and would comply with none of
their rites ; faying, that whilft he had the ufe of
his reafon, he never fpake any thing in favour of
their religion ; and that he never difowned the
proteftant faith, nor would he now. So that they
were filenced and put to fhame. There is no
reafon to think that thefe two women were any
more papifts than he ; but they are dead, and
cannot fpeak. One of the witneffes, fpoken of
in the fore-mentioned letter, told me, fhe knew
of no fuch thing, and faid Mr. Meriel told her,
that he never heard a more fervent and affection-
ate prayer than one which Efther Jones made a
little before her death. I am verily perfuaded,
that he calls that prayer to God, fo full of affection and confeffion, the confeffion made by her
of the fins of her whole life. Thefe two women
always in their health, and fo in their ficknefs,
oppofed all popifh principles, as all that knew
them can teftify, fo long as they could be permitted to go and fpeak with them. One of thefe
women was taken from the eaftward, and the
other, namely, Efther Jones, from Northampton.

In the beginning of March, 1706, Mr. Sheldon came again to Canada, with letters from
his

his excellency our governour, at which time I was a few days at Quebec. And when I was there, one night about ten o'clock, there was an earthquake, that made a report like a cannon, and made the houfes to tremble : It was heard and felt many leagues, all along the ifland of St. Laurence, and other places. When Mr. Sheldon came the fecond time, the adverfaries did what they could to retard the time of our return, to gain time to feduce our young ones to popery. Such were fent away who were judged ungainable, and moft of the younger fort ftill kept. Some were ftill flattered with promifes of reward ; and great effays made to get others married among them. One was debauched, and then in twenty-four hours of time publifhed, taken into their communion and married ; but the poor foul has had time fince to lament her fin and folly, with a bitter cry ; and afks your prayers, that God of his fovereign grace would yet bring her out of the horrible pit fhe has thrown herfelf into. Her name was Rachael Storer, of Wells.

In April, one Zebediah Williams, of our town, died : He was a very hopeful and pious young man, who carried himfelf fo in his captivity, as to edify feveral of the Englifh, and recover one fallen to popery, taken the laft war ; though fome were enraged againft him on thefe accounts ; yet even the French, where he fojourned, and with whom he converfed, would fay he was a good man : One that was very prayerful to God, and ftudious and painful in reading the holy fcriptures : A man of a good underftanding, and defirable

firable converfation. In the beginning of his
laft ficknefs, he made me a vifit, (before he went
to the hofpital at Quebec,) as he had feveral
times before, to my great fatisfaction, and our
mutual confolation and comfort in our captivity.
He lived not above two miles from me, over
the river, at the ifland of St. Laurence, about fix
weeks or two months. After his death, the
French told me, Zebediah was gone to hell, and
damned : For, faid they, he has appeared, fince
his death, to one Jofeph Egerly, an Englifhman,
who was taken the laft war, in flaming fire, telling him, " he was damned for refufing to embrace the Romifh religion, when fuch pains were
ufed to bring him to the true faith, and for being
inftrumental to draw him away from the Romifh
communion, forfaking the mafs ; and was therefore now come to advertife him of his danger."
I told them, I judged it to be a popifh lie ; faying, I blefs God our religion needs no lies to uphold, maintain, and eftablifh it, as theirs did.
But they affirmed it to be true, telling me, how
God approved of their religion, and witneffed
miraculoufly againft ours. But I ftill told them,
I was perfuaded his foul was in heaven, and that
thefe reports were only devifed fables to feduce
fouls. For feveral weeks they affirmed it, telling
me, that all who came over the river from the
ifland affirmed it to be a truth. I begged of God
to blaft this hellifh defign of theirs, fo that in the
iffue it might be to render their religion more
abominable, and that they might not gain one
foul by fuch a ftratagem. After fome weeks
had paffed in fuch affertions, there came one into

H                           my

my landlord's houfe, affirming it to be a truth reported of Zebediah, faying, Jofeph Egerly had
been over the river, and told one of our neighbours this ftory. After a few hours I faw that
neighbour, and afked him whether he had feen
Egerly lately ; he faid, yes ; what news told he
to you ? None, faid he. Then I told him what
was affirmed as a truth ; he anfwered, Egerly
faid nothing like this to him, and he was perfuaded he would have told him, if there had been
any truth in it. About a week after this, came
one John Boult from the ifland of St. Laurence,
a lad taken from Newfoundland, a very ferious,
fober lad, of about feventeen years of age ; he
had often before came over with Zebediah to
vifit me. At his coming in, he much lamented
the lofs of Zebediah, and told me, " That for
feveral weeks they had told him the fame ftory,
affirming it to be a truth, and that Egerly was fo
awakened by it, as to go again to mafs every
day ;" urging him, " fince God, in fuch a
miraculous way, offered fuch conviction of the
truth of their religion, and the falfhood and danger of ours, to come over to their religion, or
elfe his damnation would be dreadfully aggravat-
ed." He faid, " he could have no reft for
them day and night," but (faid he) " I told
them their religion was contrary to the word of
God, and therefore I would not embrace it ; and
that I did not believe what they faid." And
fays he to me, " One day I was fitting in the
houfe, and Egerly came in, and I fpake to him
before the whole family (in the French tongue,
for he could not fpeak much Englifh) and afked
　　　　　　　　　　　　　　　　　　　　him

him of this ftory ; he anfwered, it is a great
falfehood, faying, he never appeared to me, nor
have I ever reported any fuch thing to any body ;
and that he had never been at mafs fince Zebediah's death." At the hearing of which, they
were filenced and put to fhame. We bleffed
God together, for difcovering their wickednefs,
and difappointing them in what they aimed at,
and prayed to God to deliver us and all the captives from delufions, and recover them who had
fallen, and fo parted. After which I took my
pen and wrote a letter to one Mr. Samuel Hill,
an Englifh captive, taken from Wells, who lived
at Quebec, and his brother Ebenezer Hill, to
make a difcovery of this lying plot, to warn them
of their danger, and affure them of the falfehood
of this report ; but the letter fell into the hands
of the priefts, and was never delivered. This
Egerly came home with us, fo that they gained
nothing but fhame by this ftratagem. God often
difappoints the crafty devices of wicked men.

In the latter end of fummer, they told me,
" they had news from New-England, by one
who had been a captive at Bofton, who faid that
the minifters at Bofton had told the French captives, that the Proteftant religion was the only
true religion ; and that as a confirmation of it,
they would raife a dead perfon to life before their
eyes, for their conviction ; and that having perfuaded one to feign himfelf dead, they came and
prayed over him, and then commanded him in
the name of Chrift, (whofe religion they kept
pure) to arife ; they called and commanded, but
he never arofe ; fo that inftead of raifing the
dead

dead, they killed the living ; which the bereaved
relations difcovered." I told them, " it was an
old lie and calumny againft Luther and Calvin,
new vamped, and that they only change the perfons and place ;" but they affirmed it to be a
truth : I told them, " I wondered they were fo
fond of a faith propagated, and then maintained
by lying words."

We were always out of hopes of being returned
before winter, the feafon proving fo cold in the
latter end of September, and were praying to God
to prepare our hearts, with an holy fubmiffion to
his holy will, to glorify his holy name in a way
of paffive obedience, in the winter. For my own
part, I was informed by feveral who came from
the city, that the lord intendant faid, if More
returned and brought word that Battis was in
prifon, he would put me into prifon, and lay me
in irons. They would not permit me to go into
the city, faying, I always did harm when I came
to the city, and if at any time I was at the city,
they would perfuade the governour to fend me
back again.

In the beginning of laft June, the fuperior of
the priefts came to the parifh where I was, and
told me, he faw I wanted my friend captain de
Beauville, and that I was ragged. But, fays he,
your obftinacy againft our religion difcourages
from providing better clothes. I told him, it
was better going in a ragged coat, than with a
ragged confcience.

In the beginning of laft June, went out an
army of five hundred Macquas and Indians, with
an intention to have fallen on fome Englifh towns
                                          down

down Connecticut river ; but lighting on a Scata-
cook Indian, who afterwards ran away in the night,
they were difcouraged ; faying, he would alarm the
whole country.    About fifty, as fome fay, or
eighty, as others, returned.    Thus God reftrained
their wrath.

When they were promifing themfelves another
winter, to draw away the Englifh to popery, came
news that an Englifh brigantine was coming, and
that the honourable capt. Samuel Appleton efq.
was coming ambaffador, to fetch off the captives,
and capt. John Bonner with him.    I cannot tell
you how the clergy and others laboured to ftop
many of the prifoners.    To fome, lib    ; to
others, money and yearly penfions, were offered,
if they would ftay.    Some they urged to tarry at
leaft till the fpring of the year, telling them, it
was fo late in the year, they would be loft by fhip-
wreck if they went now ; fome younger ones they
told, if they went home, they would be damned,
and burn in hell forever, to affright them.    Day
and night they were urging of them to ftay.
And I was threatened to be fent aboard, without
a permiffion to come afhore again, if I fhould
again difcourfe with any of the Englifh who were
turned to their religion.    At Montreal, efpecially,
all crafty endeavours were ufed to ftay the Englifh.
They told my child, if he would ftay, he fhould
have an honourable penfion from the king every
year ; and that his mafter, who was an old man,
and the richeft in Canada, would give him a great
deal ; telling him, if he returned he would be
poor, for (faid they) your father is poor, has loft
all his eftate, it was all burnt.    But he would not

H 2                                             be

be prevailed with to ſtay. Others were alſo in like manner urged to ſtay ; but God graciouſly brake the ſnare, and brought them out. They endeavoured, in the fall of the year, to prevail with my ſon to go to France, when they ſaw he would not come to their communion any more. One woman, belonging to the eaſtern parts, who had, by their perſuaſions, married an Engliſh captive, taken the laſt war, came away with her huſband, which made them ſay, they were ſorry they ever perſuaded her to turn to their religion, and then to marry : For inſtead of advancing their cauſe by it, they had weakened it ; for now they    not only loſt her, but another they thought they had made ſure of. Another wo-man, belonging to the Eaſtward, who had been flattered to their religion, to whom a bible was denied, till ſhe promiſed to embrace their religion, and then had the promiſe of it for a little time, opening her bible whilſt in the church, and preſ-ent at maſs, ſhe read the fourth chapter of Deu-teronomy, and received ſuch conviction whilſt reading, that before her firſt communion, ſhe fell off from them, and could never be prevailed with any more to be of their religion.

We have reaſon to bleſs God, who has wrought deliverance for ſo many, and yet to pray to God for a door of eſcape to be opened for the great number yet behind, not much ſhort of an hun-dred, many of whom are children, and of theſe not a few among the ſavages ; and having loſt the Engliſh tongue, will be loſt, and turn ſavages in a little time, unleſs ſomething extraordinary prevent.

The

The veſſel that came for us, in its voyage to Canada, ſtruck on a bar of ſands, and there lay in very great hazard for four tides ; and yet they ſaw reaſon to bleſs God for ſtriking there ; for had they got over that bar, they would at midnight, in a ſtorm of ſnow, have run upon a terrible ledge of rocks.

We came away from Quebec on October 25 ; and by contrary winds and a great ſtorm, we were retarded, and then driven back near the city, and had a great deliverance from ſhipwreck, the veſſel ſtriking twice on a rock in that ſtorm. But through God's goodneſs, we all arrived in ſafety at Boſton, November 21 ; the nu    r of captives fifty-ſeven, two of whom were my children. I have yet a daughter of ten yeas of age, and many neighbours, whoſe caſe beſpeaks your compaſſion, and prayers to God to gather them, being out-caſts ready to periſh.

At our arrival at Boſton, we found the kindneſſes of the Lord in a wonderful manner, in God's opening the hearts of many, to bleſs God with us and for us, wonderfully to give for our ſupplies in our needy ſtate. We are under obligations to praiſe God, for diſpoſing the hearts of ſo many to ſo great charity, and under great bonds to pray for a bleſſing on the heads, hearts and families of them, who ſo liberally and plentifully gave for our relief. It is certain, that the charity of the whole country of Canada, though moved with the doctrine of merit, does not come up to the charity of Boſton alone, where notions of merit are rejected ; but acts of charity performed out of a right chriſtian ſpirit, from a ſpirit of

thankfulneſs

thankfulnefs to God, out of obedience to God's
command, and unfeigned love and charity to
them that are of the fame family and houfehold of
faith.   The Lord grant, that all who devife fuch
liberal things, may find the accomplifhment of
the promifes made by God, in their own perfons,
and theirs after them, from generation to generation.

I SHALL annex a fhort account of the troubles beginning to arife in Canada.   On May 16, arrived a canoe at
Quebec, which brought letters from Miffifippi, written the
May preceeding, giving an account that the plague was
there ⸺nd that one hundred and fifty French, in a very
little   e, had died of it ; and that the favages, called the
Lézilouways, were very turbulent, and had with their arrows wounded a jefuit in five places, and killed a Frenchman that waited on him.   In July, news came, that the
nations up the river were engaged in a war one againft the
other, and that the French living fo among them, and trading with them, were in great danger ; that the Mitchel-
macquinas had made war with the Mizianmies, and had
killed a mendicant friar, and three other Frenchmen, and
eleven favages, at a place called the ftraits, where they are
fettling a garrifon and place for traffick ; the Mitchel-
macquinas had taken fixteen Frenchmen prifoners, and
burnt their trading houfes.   Thefe tidings made the French
very full of perplexing troubles ; but the jefuits are endeavouring to pacify them ; but the troubles, when we
came away, were rather encreafing than leffening ; for the
laft letters from the French prifoners at Mitchel-macquina
report, that the favages had fent out two companies, one of
an hundred and fifty, another of an hundred and fixty,
againft the favages at the ftraits : and they feared, they
would engage as well againft the French as the Indians.

THE END.

*Reports of* DIVINE KINDNESS *; or,*
*Remarkable Mercies should be faith-*
*fully published, for the Praise of* GOD
*the Giver ;*

SET FORTH IN A

# SERMON,

PREACHED AT BOSTON LECTURE, *December* 5, 1706.

## BY JOHN WILLIAMS,

Paſtor of the CHURCH of CHRIST in Deerfield,
ſoon after his Return from Captivity,

PSALM cvii. 13, 14, 15, 32. *He ſaved them out of their diſtreſſes. He
brought them out of darkneſs, and the ſhadow of death ; and brake their
bands in ſunder. O that men would praiſe the Lord for his goodneſs ;
and for his wonderful works to the children of men.—Let them exalt him
alſo in the congregation of the people, and praiſe him in the aſſembly of the
elders.*

PSALM xxxiv. 3. *O magnify the Lord with me, and let us exalt his
name together.*

---

LUKE VIII. 39.

*Return to thine own houſe, and ſhew how great
things* GOD *hath done unto thee.——*

THE infinitely wiſe diſpoſer of all things,
who aims at his own glory, in the govern-
ing of rational creatures, doth ſometimes bring
perſons into the depths of diſtreſs ; and then
magnify his power and grace in raiſing them up
out of their afflictions : And in many reſpects, by
ſuch things, he has a deſign of advancing his own
honour and glory in the world. We find in the
context, a perſon in a very doleful, diſtreſſed condition : He ſeems to be forſaken of God, and
made

made a poffeffion and dwelling place of evil fpirits, deprived of all human comforts and delights,
made to poffefs forrow and pain to fuch a degree,
as to be a common fubject or theme of difcourfe
for all men to relate doleful things about. And
afterward, God, in very remarkable and wonderful works of power and mercy, not only gives
releafe from his forrowful poffeffion, but he is
fitting at the feet of Jefus, cloathed, and in his
right mind. Now this was done for the declarative and manifeftative glory and honour of God.
For when this man, for whom fuch great things
had be done, petitions Chrift that he may abide
wit in, to hear from him, and pay his refpects
to him ; he receives commandment, to be glorifying the power and mercy of God, in declaring to
others what great things God had done for him.

1. A fubject of great mercy ; or a perfon
fpoken of, for whom God had done great things,
beftowed eminent mercies.

2. A particular and fpecial command from
Chrift, to be glorifying God in relating to others,
what mercies he had been the fubject of.

3. His obedience to the great command of Chrift.
He went and publifhed the great things done for
him by Chrift; fo that from the command of Chrift,
and his obedience to it, for which he is commended, you may obferve this doctrinal conclufion.

DOCT. It well becomes thofe who have had eminent mercies, to be fhewing to others what
   great things God has done for them.

The holy fcriptures, in many places, confirm
this truth. See Exod. xii. 25, 26, 27. *And it*
*fhall*

*shall come to pass, when ye be come to the land, which
the Lord will give you, according as he hath promised,
that ye shall keep this service.   And it shall come to
pass, when your children shall say unto you, what
mean you by this service ?  That ye shall say, it is the
sacrifice of the Lord's passover, who passed over the
houses of the children of Israel in Egypt, when he
smote the Egyptians, and delivered our houses.* Exod.
xiii. 8, 10. *And thou shalt shew thy son in that day,
saying, this is done because of that which the Lord
did unto me, when I came forth out of Egypt.   Thou
shalt therefore keep this ordinance in his seafon from
year to year.*  Pfal. lxxviii. 3, 4. *Which we have
heard and known, and our fathers have told us ; we
will not hide them from their children, shewing to the
generation to come the praises of the Lord ; and his
strength, and his wonderful works that he hath done.*
In the profecution and handling of this truth,
confider,

I.  They who have had mercies, have had them
from God.   God is the beftower and giver of all
our good things : All our mercies come to us by
a divine providence, and ordering ; not by cafu-
alty or accident :  Neither are they of our own
procuring and purchafing, or others, fo as to ex-
clude the providential difpofing of God.   It is
God who returns the captivity of Zion, Pfalm
cxxvi. begin. *When the Lord turned again the captivity of Zion, we were like them that dream : Then was
our mouth filled with laughter, and our tongue with
singing.   Then said they among the heathen, the Lord
hath done great things for them.   The Lord hath done
great things for us ; whereof we are glad : Turn again
our captivity, O Lord.*  The very heathen acknowledge

edge the good things beſtowed upon, and done for
the church, to be from God ; and God's own people acknowledge him for the mercies granted,
and humbly ſupplicate mercies from him for the
future. It is God who gathers the out-caſts of
Iſrael : It is he who takes away the captives of
the mighty, the prey of the terrible ; who con-
tends with them that contend with us, and ſaves
our children. It is God who diſperſeth and
gathers again : Therefore the pſalmiſt, Pſal. ciii.
begin. calls upon his ſoul to bleſs the Lord,
and not to forget all his benefits ; and ſaith, *It is
God who forgiveth all thy iniquities, who healeth all
thy diſeaſes : Who redeemeth thy life from deſtruc-
tion, who crowneth thee with loving kindneſs and
tender mercies,* &c. Sometimes God, in a more
immediate and extraordinary way and manner,
confers bleſſings and mercies ; ſometimes in a
more ordinary and mediate way ; but his providence is to be acknowledged in all : Not one
ſingle mercy comes to us, without a commiſſion
from that God by whom our very hairs are num-
bered.

II. It well becomes thoſe who have had eminent mercies, to be ſhowing to others what great
things God hath done for them. Therefore you
find the holy pſalmiſt calling upon others, to give
a liſtening ear, whilſt he makes a narration of the
ſalvations he had from God, Pſal. lxvi. 16. *Come
and hear, all you that fear God, and I will declare
what he hath done for my ſoul.*

1ſt *Reaſon.* Becauſe God aimed at the advancement of his own honour and glory, in the
giving and dealing out of theſe mercies. God
makes

makes and difpofeth all things for his own honour and glory. All works of providence are fome way or other to advance the honour and glory of God in the world. The glory of his power, wifdom, mercy, juftice and holinefs, are fome way or other advanced in a declarative and manifeftative way and manner. Now it well becomes us to fall in with the defign of God, and in an active manner to be giving him glory. That God defigns to have glory given to him, is evident from Pfal. l. 15. *And call upon me in the day of trouble, I will deliver thee, and thou fhalt glorify me.* Exod. vii. 5. *And the Egyptians fhall know that I am the Lord, when I ftretch forth mine hand upon Egypt, and bring out the children of Ifrael from among them.* God has a defign to magnify his power, mercy and covenant faithfulnefs, in the eyes of the world.

*2d Reafon.* Becaufe God has given us direct precepts, and pofitive commands, in this way, to be glorifying of him. God is our Lord and lawgiver, and he requires, that among other ways of fhowing forth his praifes, we do it by rehearfing his praife-worthy acts to the children of men: So that in obedience to God, and anfwering that high and noble end we were made for, it is requifite that in this way we glorify God. It is enough, that the great God, who hath taken us into covenant relation to himfelf, has enjoined us to fhew forth his praifes, in rehearfing to others the falvations and favours we have been the fubjects of. The forementioned fcriptures, with many others that might be enumerated, fufficiently demonftrate, that God calls for our thankful acknowledgments in this way ; and upon the

I                                            account

account of this being so agreeable to the revealed and perceptive will of God, the pſalmiſt expreſſeth himſelf, as in Pſal. cxlv. 4, 5, 6. *One generation ſhall praiſe thy works to another, and ſhall declare thy mighty acts. I will ſpeak of the glorious honour of thy majeſty, and of thy wondrous works. And men ſhall ſpeak of the might of thy terrible acts: And I will declare thy greatneſs. They ſhall abundantly utter the memory of thy great goodneſs; and ſhall ſing of thy righteouſneſs.* Verſes 10, 11, 12. *All thy works ſhall praiſe thee, O Lord; and thy ſaints ſhall bleſs thee. They ſhall ſpeak of the glory of thy kingdom and talk of thy power: To make known to the ſons of men his mighty acts, and the glorious majeſty of his kingdom.*

3d *Reaſon.* Becauſe hereby they will ſtir up others to bleſs God with them, and for them. A truly gracious ſoul finds by experience, that he can do but a little in glorifying God, and finds how far he falls ſhort of the rule of duty in ſo reaſonable a ſervice as glorifying God. And be-ing enlarged in deſires that the glory due to God might be given him, doth call upon others to join with him in this heavenly ſervice of praiſing God; and therefore tells them what great things God has done. Pſalm xxxiv. 2, 3, 4, 6. *My ſoul ſhall make her boaſt in the Lord: The humble ſhall hear thereof, and be glad. O magnify the Lord with me, and let us exalt his name together. I ſought the Lord, and he heard me; and delivered me from all my fears. This poor man cried, and the Lord heard him; and ſaved him out of all his troubles.* When Moſes told his father-in-law Jethro, the great things God had done for Iſrael, he glorifies God

God on their behalf, Exod. xviii. 8, &c. *And Moses told his father-in-law, all that the Lord had done unto Pharaoh, and to the Egyptians for Israel's sake, and all the travail that had come upon them by the way, and how the Lord delivered them. And Jethro rejoiced for all the goodness which the Lord had done to Israel; whom he had delivered out of the hand of the Egyptians. And Jethro said, blessed be the Lord, who hath delivered you out of the hand of the Egyptians, and out of the hand of Pharaoh, who hath delivered the people from under the hand of the Egyptians. Now I know that the Lord is greater than all gods: For in the thing wherein they dealt proudly, he was above them.* By this means, thanks will be given to God by many: As many have been praying to God for them, so many will be praising and blessing God with them and for them.

*4th Reason.* Because hereby they will oftentimes be advised and counselled how to improve such mercies to the glory of God. We are conscious to ourselves of so much blindness, ignorance, and darkness, that we cannot but own it a great thing to be in a way for the best counsel, what to do with our mercies, and what and how to return to God for them. Now the publishing the great things done by God for us, puts others in a capacity to be advising and telling us what temptations we may expect to meet with, and what will be needful on our part to avoid temptations, and how to over-come; they will be counselling us, how to be in a way of rendering to the Lord according to the benefits done unto us; what duties God looks for the performance of, and directions how to do duty. In a
word,

word, we may be counselled how to order our
whole conversation so as God may have glory,
and our good purposes of honouring and glorifying God with our mercies, established. Prov. xx.
18. *Every purpose is established by counsel.* When
Moses had told Jethro what great things God
had done for Israel, he saith, Exod. xviii. 19.
*Hearken now unto my voice, I will give thee counsel,
and God shall be with thee,* &c.

*5th Reason.* Because hereby they will be instrumental to put others upon trusting God,
making him their hope and refuge in an evil day.
Others will be excited to a seeking refuge under
the shadow of his wings, Psal. xliv. begin. *We
have heard with our ears, O God, our fathers have
told us, what work thou didst in their days, in the
times of old. How thou didst drive out the heathen,*
&c. And then it is said, *Thou art my king, O
God: Command deliverances for Jacob. Through
thee will we push down our enemies: Through thy
name will we tread them under that rise up against
us. For I will not trust in my bow, neither shall my
sword save me. In God we boast all the day long.*
Others that have heard, will say, such and such
an one was thus exercised, and God appeared for
them, and put songs of praise to the Lord into
their mouths ; we will commit our case to God
too ; we will both hope and quietly wait for
God's salvation too. Your telling others, how
you have found God a prayer-hearing God, will
encourage them, prayer-wise, to be committing
their distressed and difficult cases to him. What
an honour to be instrumental to any soul's comfort, and God's honour ; agreeable to this is
that

dry, to live, and can in ways unthought of by you, both recover them after they have fallen, and return them again. The adverfaries have fometimes pretended miracles for the confirmation of their religion, that they might feduce to popery; in fallacious ways caufed reports that fome captives died papifts; that one appeared in flames of fire to bear a teftimony againft the Proteftant religion; but God has, in his wife providence, made known their falfehoods and lies.

They have fought to perfuade fome, by fums of money, to change their religion, offering honour and advancement to them at the fame time; but God has enabled them to refift and hate fuch allurements.

The reading the fourth chapter of Deuteronomy, a means of recovering one from popery.

God has made fome, with an heroical, yea with a right chriftian courage, to welcome death. Oh let every one get fuch a preparednefs for death, that a fudden death may not be a terror!

God has made fome, by the want of fanctuary mercies, to fet an higher value upon the ordinances of Jefus Chrift. Oh learn to prize and improve them, left God teach you, by the briars and thorns of the wildernefs, the worth of them, and make you weep when you fit down at the rivers of Babylon.

God has ftrengthened fome to ftand, when they have not only been threatened with all cruelties if they refufed, but when the hatchet has been lifted up, with a threatening of fpeedy death in cafe of refufal. Oh let every one truft in God, who is a feafonable help and a prefent refuge!

INSTRUCTION

INSTRUCTION II. How they are to blame, that do not regard and take notice of the works of God, nor treasure up the remembrance of them in their minds. How soon are mercies like to be forgotten ; the psalmist says, *Forget not all his benefits*. It was the great sin of the Israel-ites of old, that they soon forgat God's wonder-ous works. The holy God gave order, that his people should erect stones of remembrance, that his wonderful works of mercy to his people might not be forgotten ; yea, commanded pa-rents to tell their children, from generation to generation, what great things he had done for them. How are they then to blame that say, *They bless God for their mercies*, and do not re-hearse the praise-worthy works of divine provi-dence to others.

USE II. To direct such, who have received great and eminent mercies from God, in this way of making known to others the wonders of mer-cy to them, to be praising God. It is one way very proper and agreeable to the revealed will of God : You must watch against all vain ostentation.

USE III. Of EXHORTATION. To all who have, in a more peculiar way and manner, been casting off the effects and fruits of divine bounty and goodness, to be declaring what great things God has done for them.

Therefore, 1. Beware of all manner of pride. Sometimes men cannot declare the great works of God done for them, without making known their own weakness, and therefore are silent, and hold their peace ; they had rather God should lose his glory, than they any of their credit or esteem.

eſteem. But the holy pſalmiſt ſays, *His feet had well nigh ſlipt ; yea, that in his haſte he had ſaid, all men are liars ;* and that one day he ſhould ſurely periſh ; take ſhame to himſelf, that he might magnify the preventing and delivering grace and goodneſs of God. Sometimes men's pride makes them ſo admire their own parts and contrivances, as to over-look the works of divine providence ; they ſacrifice to their own net, and burn incenſe to their own drag ; and ſay they have ſo much learning and knowledge, that they could eaſily anſwer arguments to ſeduce them to popery ; and ſo do not ſee and acknowledge the goodneſs of God, in preſerving and keeping them.

2. Beware of a ſtupid, ſenſeleſs, ſlothful ſpirit. The works of God are ſought out of them that have pleaſure in them. Some will not be at the pains to recollect the paſſages of divine provi-dence ; will not commit them to writing, or to their memories, and therefore ſoon forget them ; they never wiſely obſerve the heightening cir-cumſtances of their mercies.

Conſider, 3. How heavenly an employ and ſervice it is, to be glorifying and praiſing God. It will be one part of the work of heaven, to be telling of the wonderful works of God towards us. Begin ſuch an heavenly employ on earth. Hereby you will alſo intereſt yourſelves in the prayers of others : To have many prayers going daily to God for you, how great a favour is it ! Others hearing what mercies you have had, will bear you upon their hearts when at the throne of grace, that you may ſuitably improve ſuch mercies.

The

The glorifying God is the greateſt and chiefeſt concern of gracious ſouls ; and the glorifying of God here, is the way to be glorified by, and with God forever. The not glorifying God is very diſpleaſing to him, and a way to deprive ourſelves of the ſweet and comfort of our mercies. God accounts forgetting of mercies, a forgetting himſelf.

### END OF THE SERMON.

# A P P E N D I X.

*Drawn up and ſent to the Rev. Mr. Prince, by the Rev. Mr. Stephen Williams, of Springfield, who on February 29th, 1703-4. was, with his Rev. father, Mr. John Williams, of Deerfield, carried captive into Canada, but returned, and was educated at Harvard College.*

### Names of thoſe Perſons who were taken Captive at Deerfield, Feb. 29th, 1703-4.

Mary Alexander,
Mary Alexander, jun.
Joſeph Alexander, *ran away the firſt night.*
Sarah Allen,
Mary Allis,
Thomas Baker,
Simon Beaumont,
Hannah Beaumont,
* Hephzibah Belding,
John Bridgman, *ran away in the meadow.*
Nathaniel Brooks,
* Mary Brooks,
† Mary Brooks, jun.
† William Brooks,
Abigail Brown,
Benjamin Burt,
John Burt,
Sarah Burt,
Hannah Carter,

* Hannah Carter, jun.
† Mercy Carter,
+ Samuel Carter,
† John Carter,
Ebenezer Carter,
* Marah Carter,
John Catlin,
Ruth Catlin,
* Elizabeth Corſe,
† Elizabeth Corſe, jun
† Daniel Crowfoot,
† Abigail Denio,
Sarah Dickinſon,
Joſeph Eaſtman,
Mary Field,
John Field,
† Mary Field, jun.
* Mary Frary,
Thomas French,
* Mary French,
Thomas French, jun.

Mary French, jun.
† Freedom French,
† Martha French,
Abigail French,
† Mary Harris,
† Samuel Haſtings,
* Elizabeth Hawks,
Mehuman Hinſdel,
Mary Hinſdel,
Jacob Hix, *died at Cowaſs*
*Deacon David Hoit, died at Cowaſs.*
Abigail Hoit,
Jonathan Hoit,
Sarah Hoit,
† Ebenezer Hoit,
* Abigail Hoit, jun.
Elizabeth Hull,
† Thomas Hurſt,
† Ebenezer Hurſt,
* Benoni Hurſt,

Sarah Hurst,
Sarah Hurst, jun
Elizabeth Hurst,
† Hannah Hurst,
Martin Kellogg,
Martin Kellogg, jun.
Joseph Kellogg,
† Joanna Kellogg,
Rebecca Kellogg,
John Marsh,
Sarah Multoon,
* Philip Multoon,
* Frank, a negro.
* Mehitable Nims,
Ebenezer Nims,
† Abigail Nims,
Joseph Petty,
Sarah Petty,

Lydia Pomroy,
Joshua Pomroy,
* Esther Pomroy,
Samuel Price,
† Jemima Richards,
† Josiah Riseing,
Hannah Shelden,
Ebenezer Shelden,
Remembrance Shelden,
Mary Shelden,
John Stebbins,
Dorothy Stebbins,
John Stebbins, jun.
Samuel Stebbins,
† Ebenezer Stebbins,
† Joseph Stebbins,
† Thankful Stebbins,
† Elizabeth Stevens,

Ebenezer Warner,
* Waitstill Warner,
† Waitstill Warner, jun.
Sarah Warner,
Rev. John Williams,
* Mrs. Eunice Williams,
Samuel Williams,
Stephen Williams,
† Eunice Williams, jun.
Esther Williams,
Warham Williams,
John Weston,
Judah Wright.
    Three Frenchmen who
had lived in the town for
some time, and came from
Canada, were also taken.

NOTE. Where there is this sign * against the person's name, it is to signify they were killed after they went out of town : And this mark † is
to signify that they are still absent from their native country.

---

*Names of those who were slain at that time in or near the town.*

SLAIN IN THE TOWN.

DAVID Alexander,
Thomas Carter,
John Catlin,
Jonathan Catlin,
Sarah Field,
Samson Frary,
John French,
Alice Hawks,
John Hawks, jun. and
    his wife,
Thankful Hawks,
John Hawks,
Martha Hawks,

Samuel Hinsdale,
Joseph Ingersol,
Jonathan Kellogg,
Philip Matloon's wife
    and child,
Parthena, a negro.
Henry Nims,
Mary Nims, *
Mercy Nims,
Mehitable Nims,
Sarah Price,
Mercy Root,
Thomas Shelden,

Mrs. Shelden,
Mercy Shelden,
Samuel Smead's wife and
    two children,
Elizabeth Smead,
Martin Smith,
Serg. Benoni Stebbins,
Andrew Stevens,
Mary Wells,
John Williams, jun.
Jerusha Williams.

SLAIN IN THE MEADOW.

SAMUEL Allis,
Serg. Boltwood,
Robert Boltwood,

Joseph Catlin,
Samuel Foot,
David Hoit, jun.

Jonathan Ingram,
Serg. Benjamin Wait
Nathaniel Warner.

* These three it was supposed were burnt in the cellar.

---

*An account of the mischief done by the enemy in Deerfield, from
    beginning of its settlement to the death of the Rev Mr.
    John Williams, in June, 1729.*

THE enemy beset the place, and killed one
    Eggleston, September 1, 1675.

    The Indians fell upon the people as they were going
to publick worship, on Sept. 12. 1675, and wounded one
    Harrington in the neck, but the wound did not
K                                                           prove

prove mortal. One man was drove into the swamp, taken and killed.

3. Captain Lothrop and company were slain at Muddy brook (alias) Bloody brook, on Sept. 18, 1675.

4. The *fall fight* (as it is called) was on May 18, 1676, when a great slaughter was made of the enemy, but Capt. Turner and 37 men were lost. There were many remarkables, relating to this affair, (as related by Jonathan Wells, Esq. who was present) which are not taken notice of by Mr. Hubbard, or Dr. Mather.

5. Sept. 19, 1677. John Root was killed, and Serg. Plympton, Quintin Stockwell, and Benoni Stebbins, were taken captive, but Stebbins made his escape from them and got home. This was after they began to settle the place a second time; for upon capt. Lothrop's loss, the town was deserted for some time; but this year, 1677, they began to build again. Serg. Plympton was accounted a gracious man; he was burnt by the Indians, and the Indians obliged one Dickinson, taken at Hatfield, to lead him to the stake: The manner of burning was this; they covered him with dry bark, set it on fire, then they quenched the fire, and anon firing it again. He went cheefully to the stake, &c. The town was deserted for some time: In 1684, they returned again to settle the town.

6. June, 1693. The widow Hepzibah Wells and her three daughters were knocked on the head and scalped, two of them died, but the other lived; at the same time Thomas Broughton was killed, and his wife, great with child, and three of their children.

7. On October 13, 1693. Martin Smith was taken, and carried to Canada, from whence he returned after some years.

8. Sept. 15, 1694. Monsieur Caltreen, with a number of Indians, beset the fort, but were beat off: Daniel Severance (a lad) was killed in the meadow; and John Beaumont, and Richard Lyman, soldiers in the fort, were wounded, but recovered. Mrs. Hannah Beaumont and some children who were her scholars, were remarkably preserved: As they ran from the house to the fort, the enemy fired many shot at them, and the bullets whistled about their ears; but none of them were hurt, although some of the enemy were very near them.

9. August 18, 1695. Mr. Joseph Barnard was fired upon by the enemy, and his horse was shot down: He himself

himfelf was wounded in the body, one wrift fhivered to pieces, his other hand wounded ; but yet through the bravery of Godfry Nims, and others with him, he was brought into the town, and lived till Sept. 6, and then died, greatly lamented, &c.

10. Sept. 16, 1696.  John Gillet and John Smead, were hunting up green river ; the Indians came upon them, and took Gillet, but Smead made his efcape ; the enemy left two or three men with Gillet, and the reft came along to the town, and affaulted Daniel Belding's houfe, took Mr. Belding, his fon Nathaniel, and daughter Efther, captive : Killed his wife and three children, and wounded Samuel and Abigail, but they recovered, although Samuel had a hatchet ftuck in his head, and fome of his brains came out at the wound.

11. July, 1698.  Nathaniel Pomroy was killed, being with a party of men that went up the river after fome Indians that had done mifchief at Hatfield : At the fame time Samuel Dickinfon, and one ———— Charly, were retaken from the enemy.  This is related by Dr. Cotton Mather, in his hiftory of the ten years war, &c.

12. October 8, 1703.  Zebediah Williams and John Nims, were taken captive, and carried to Canada ; Williams died there ; Nims, with fome others, made their efcape, and got home to Deerfield, in 1705.

13. The town was taken February 29, 1703.4.

14. May 11, 1704.  John Allen and his wife were killed at a place called the Barrs.

15. Serg. John Hawks, riding on the road, was fired at by the enemy, and wounded in the hand, but got off to Hatfield, and his wound was healed, &c.  This was in the fummer of 1704.

16. July 19, 1704.  Thomas Ruffell was killed by the enemy, north of the town.

17. Auguft, 1708.  A fcout went up to the white river, and as they returned, were fired upon by the enemy, and one man, whofe name was Barber, was killed ; and he killed the Indian that killed him.  Martin Kellogg, jun. was taken captive, and the reft efcaped.

18. Oct. 26, 1708.  E. Field was killed near muddy brook.

19. Mehuman Hinfdale was taken captive as he was driving his team from Northampton.  This was April 11, 1709 : The fecond time of his captivity : He was carried

to Canada, and from thence to France, and got to England, and from thence home, &c.

20. May, 1709. Lieut. John Wells, and John Burt, were loft in a fkirmifh with the enemy on the French river, after they had been, with others, as far as Lake Champlain, and killed fome of the enemy.

21. Jofeph Cleffon and John Arms were taken June 22, 1709, and the next day Jonathan Williams was killed, and Matthew Cleffon mortally wounded ; and Jieut. Thomas Taylor and Ifaac Matloon were wounded, but recovered.

22. July 30, 1712. Serg. Samuel Taylor, and others, were fent out as a fcout to the north river, they were attacked by the enemy, and Samuel Androfs was killed ; Jonathan Barrett was wounded in the fide, and then taken ; one William Sandford was alfo taken, the reft got home, &c. The prifoners were carried to Canada, where they met lieut. Samuel Williams, (who was then at Canada with a flag of truce), who ranfomed them from the Indians, and brought them home : They were abfent but about two months.

23. June 27, 1724. Ebenezer Shelden, Thomas Colton, and Jeremiah Englifh, (a friend Indian), were killed on the road beyond the green river houfes ; and it was fuppofed the enemy received fome damage from fome of our forces, who came upon them fpeedily, &c.

24. July 10, 1724. Lieut. Timothy Childs and Samuel Allen, were fhot upon and wounded, as they were returning from their labour in the field, but they efcaped, and were healed of their wounds.

25. Auguft 25, 1725. Deacon Field, deacon Childs, and others, were going up to green river farms, and were ambufhed by the Indians, but they difcovered the Indians ; and John Wells difcharged his gun at an Indian, who fell : The Indians fired at them, and wounded deacon Samuel Field, the ball paffing through the right hypocondria, cutting off three plaits of the myfenteria, which hung out of the wound, in length almoft two inches, which was cut off even with the body, the bullet paffing between the loweft and the next rib, cutting, at its going forth, the loweft rib : His hand being clofe to the body when the ball came forth, it entered at the root of the heel of the thumb, cutting the bone of the fore finger, and, refting between the fore and fecond finger, was cut out, and all the wounds were cured in lefs than five weeks, by doctor Thomas Haftings.

# APPENDIX.

*By the* Rev. JOHN TAYLOR, *the present minister of the Gospel,
in Deerfield ; containing some account of the mischief done by
the enemy, in Deerfield, and its vicinity, from the death of the
Rev. Mr.* WILLIAMS, *to the conclusion of the last French war.*

THE readers of this appendix, will probably feel
desirous of knowing the reasons, why, in many things, I
have been so general ; only having given a brief statement
of facts ; and in others, have been more particular.  I trust,
it will be a sufficient apology to observe, that I have done
it for want of better documents.  Most of the facts mentioned, I have taken from the minutes of some gentlemen,
who kept them, only for their own satisfaction, and were
not particular ; and now, the distance of time, precludes the
possibility of obtaining such an account of circumstances,
as may be depended on.

One reason, of my adding this appendix, is, I suppose
that it will not be disagreeable to any who were desirous
that the narrative should be reprinted, especially the descend-
ants of those who were either killed, wounded, or captivated ; and for this reason I have been careful also to mention the names of such.

Another reason is, I think that every vestige of history,
which respects the early settlement of a country, should be
preserved, for the satisfaction of future generations.

THE last account of mischief, mentioned in the former
appendix, done by the enemy in this part of the country,
was in August, 1725.  This year, terminated the war.
A treaty of peace was held at Boston, by commissioners
from the General Court, and the chiefs of the Indian
tribes ; at which, articles were signed, and a long peace ensued.

There appeared, for many years, an unusually pacific
spirit among the Indians ; probably in consequence of some
acts of the General Court, favourable to them in their trade.
It was thought, that they never again would have been
disposed to hostilities, had they not been under the immediate influence of French interest.

War was declared between France and England, March,
1744.  The first year of the war, no Indians made their
K 2                                    appearance

appearance in this part of the country : They had found by experience, that to maintain an open trade with the English, was greatly for their interest ; and consequently at first, entered into the war with reluctance.

The first mischief that I can obtain an account of, done by the enemy, in this part of the country, in the course of this war, was in July, 1745 ; when a few Indians came to a place called the great meadow, about 16 miles above fort Dummer, on Connecticut river ; two of whom, captivated William Phips, as he was hoeing his corn. After having taken, and led him about half a mile, they made a stand ; and as the Indians afterwards informed, one of them having laid down his gun, and gone a few rods, for the purpose of fetching something he had left, on his return, Phips took up the Indian's gun, fired upon, and killed him ; then fell upon the other with his hoe, struck him down, and bruised him, until he supposed he was dead ; he then attempted to make his escape, but unfortunately, three more of the enemy came upon him, and killed him.

The same month, deacon Josiah Fisher, was killed, and scalped at a place called the upper Ashwelot.

October 11. The fort at the great meadow, was attacked by a large party of French and Indians ; the attack was bold, and furious, but without success. No lives were lost. Nehemiah Howe was taken captive, and carried to Quebec, where he soon died. The enemy on their return, met one David Rugg, with another person, passing down Connecticut river in a canoe ; Rugg they killed, and scalped, the other person, with some difficulty, made his escape.

I can find no farther account of mischief done by the enemy, in this part of the country, in the year 1745, but in 46 they began in season, and the sufferings of the people were very considerable.

In April, the enemy made their appearance at No. 4, (now Charleston), which was then the most northern settlement, on Connecticut river ; capt. John Spafford, Isaac Parker, and Stephen Farnsworth, being at a little distance from the fort, were captivated, and carried to Canada.

The same month, a party of Indians ambushed the road, between Northfield and Lunenburgh, and killed Joshua Holton.

On the 23d of the same month, a large party of the enemy, came to the upper Ashwelot, with a design to have taken the fort by surprise, but being discovered by a person

who

who was providentially at that time at a little distance from
the garrison, they were disconcerted ; an action however
ensued, which continued for some time ; the enemy finally
withdrew.   In this action, John Bullard was killed, Nathan
Blake was captivated, and the wife of Daniel M'Kinne,
being out of the fort, was overtaken and stabbed.   Before
the enemy retired, they burnt several buildings, which was
supposed to have been done, not so much for the sake of
mischief, as to conceal their dead ; there being many human bones afterwards found among the ashes.

In the beginning of May, the enemy again appeared at
No. 4 ; a few people were near a barn, about sixty rods
from the fort, when they were fired upon by a considerable
body who had concealed themselves in the barn.   Seth Put-
nam, a soldier belonging to the fort, was killed ; whilst the
enemy were endeavouring to scalp him, major Willard,
commander of the garrison, with two soldiers, ran near to
them undiscovered, and fired upon them, upon which they
retreated with great haste.   The Indians afterwards reported to the prisoners in Canada, that at this time two of
their number were mortally wounded, and died soon after.

May 6, a large party of Indians made an attempt upon
the fort at Falltown ; (now Bernardston), a person about
forty rods from the fort discovering them, gave information
to another farther distant than himself ; by this the enemy
found they were discovered, and ran immediately to the
fort ; an attack commenced, which continued for some
time, and though there were but three soldiers in the fort,
they defended it till the enemy withdrew.   John Burk was
slightly wounded, one house was burnt, and about ten cattle were killed.   Two Indians were mortally wounded, who
died soon after their return.

On the same day, Serg. John Hawks, and John Miles,
were fired upon by two Indians, as they were riding out
from fort Massachusetts, and were both wounded : Miles
made his escape to the fort ; Hawks fought for some time,
and as afterwards appeared, might have taken them both
prisoners had he understood their language ; they asked him
for quarter before he turned to make his escape.

10th.  Five of that party of Indians, who the day before
had been at Falltown fort, ambushed the road at Colrain.
Matthew Clark, with his wife and daughter, together
with two soldiers were fired upon, a few rods from the fort ;
Clark

Clark was killed, and his wife and daughter were wounded ;
one of the foldiers returning the fire, killed one of the enemy,
which gave them a check,. and he brought the wounded
into the fort.

A few days after, about twenty men were out, fifty or
fixty rods from the fort, at No. 4, viewing the place where
Parker was killed on the 2d of the month, and before they
difcovered an enemy, they were fired upon by a large body
of Indians, who immediately endeavoured to cut off their
communication with the fort ; capt. Stevens, commander
of the garrifon, came out with a body of men for their
relief, a fevere action commenced, which continued for
fome time ; at laft the enemy fled ; and as was fuppofed
with confiderable lofs.    Capt. Stevens loft three, viz.
Aaron Lyon, Peter Perrin, and Jofeph Marcy ; he had four
wounded, and one taken captive.

June 11. A party of the enemy again appeared at fort
Maffachufetts ; a number of men being at fome diftance
from the fort, were attacked, and a fkirmifh enfued : The
enemy fled, after fuftaining the fire but a few moments.
Elifha Nims, and Gerfhom Hawks were wounded ; and
Benj. Teuter was captivated.    One of the enemy was killed.

19th· A large body of the enemy again appeared at No.
4 ; capt. Stevens, and capt. Brown, marching with about
fifty men from the fort into the meadow, were ambufhed ;
the enemy were difcovered before they fired : Stevens began the attack, and a fevere action enfued ;. after fome
time the enemy were repulfed, and retreated in great hafte
and confufion.    Capt. Stevens loft none`on the fpot.    Jed-
ediah Winchel was mortally wounded, and died foon after.
David Parker, Jonathan Stanhope, and Noah Heaton were
alfo wounded, but recovered.

20th. A party of about twenty Indians came to Bridgman's fort, about two miles below fort Dummer, and fell
upon a number of men who were at work in the meadow.
In this fkirmifh William Robins and James Parker were killed ; John Beaumont and Daniel How were taken captive ;
M. Gilfon, and Patrick Ray were wounded, but recovered.

July 3. The enemy waylaid a mill in Hinfdale ; colonel
Willard having come to the mill with a guard of about 20
men, for the purpofe of grinding, and having placed his
guards, they were foon fired upon ; the col. calling to his
men with great earneftnefs to fall upon them, gave them
                                                        fuch

such a fright, that they fled, leaving behind them their packs, and provisions, to the value of 40l. old tenor.

28th. David Morrison, of Colrain, was taken captive, near one of the garrisons.

August 3. A body of the enemy appeared at No. 4; suspicions of their approach were excited by the yelling of dogs. A scout was sent out from the fort, and had proceeded but a few rods before they were fired on. Ebenezer Philips was killed; the remainder made their escape to the fort; the enemy surrounded the garrison, and endeavoured, for three days, to take it; but finding their efforts ineffectual, they withdrew, after having burnt several buildings, and killed all the cattle, horses, &c. which they could find.

11th. Benj. Wright, of Northfield, riding in the woods, was fired on, and mortally wounded; he died in a few hours.

17th. Ezekiel Wallingford was killed, and scalped, at a place called Poquiag. The same day, a person by the name of Bills, was killed, and scalped, on the road between Deerfield, and Colrain, or Bernardston.

20th An army of about nine hundred French and Indians, under command of gen. de Vaudreuil, made an attack upon fort Massachusetts. The fort was commanded by col. Hawks, who, unfortunately, was not in a situation to defend it against such a force, having but thirty-three persons, men, women, and children, in the fort; and being miserably provided with ammunition; with great fortitude, he defended it for twenty eight hours; and had not his ammunition failed, it is probable he never would have given up the fort. He was, finally, necessitated to capitulate; and he offered such articles as were accepted by de Vaudreuil. One special article in this capitulation, was, that none of the prisoners should be delivered into the hands of the Indians; the next day, however, Vaudreuil divided the prisoners, and delivered them one half, in open violation, and contempt of the article. * The Indians immediately killed one, who, by reason of sickness, was unable to travel. The prisoners were, in general, treated with civility, most of whom were afterwards redeemed. Col. Hawks lost but one man in the siege. Gen. de Vaudreuil, according to the best

* General de Vaudreuil's plea for this breach of faith, was, the danger of mutiny in his army, the Indians being irritated to a great degree, on account of their being cut off, by the capitulation, from all the profits of the conquest. But, how far this plea was a justification of such perfidy, I leave to the judicious to determine.

beſt accounts the priſoners could obtain, loſt forty-five, who were either killed outright, or died of their wounds.

Immediately after the capture of the fort, a party of about fifty Indians came on, for the purpoſe of making depredations upon Deerfield. They came firſt upon a hill, at the ſouth weſt corner of the ſouth meadow, where they diſcovered ten, or twelve, men and children at work, in a ſituation, in which they might all, with eaſe, be made priſoners. Had they ſucceeded in their deſign, which was, to obtain priſoners, rather than ſcalps, it is probable that events would not have been ſo diſaſterous as they proved. They were diſconcerted by the following circumſtance : Mr. Eleazer Hawks was out that morning a fowling, and was providentially at the foot of the hill, at the time the enemy came down ; they, ſeeing him, ſuppoſed they were diſcovered; and immediately fired upon him, killed, and ſcalped him. This gave an alarm to the people in the meadow, ſome of whom were but a few rods diſtant. The enemy were now ſenſible, that what they did muſt be done with diſpatch. Accordingly they ruſhed into the meadow, fired on Simeon Amſden, a lad, and killed him, beheaded, and ſcalped him. Mr. Samuel Allen, John Sadler, and Adonijah Gillet, ran a few rods, and made a ſtand, under the bank of the river, where they were attacked with fury, and fought for a little time with great bravery ; they were, however, ſoon overpowered with numbers. Allen and Gillet fell. Sadler, finding himſelf alone, ran acroſs the river, and made his eſcape, amidſt a ſhower of balls. Whilſt this was paſſing, Oliver Amſden was purſued a few rods, overtaken, and ſtabbed, after having his hands and fingers cut in pieces, by endeavouring to defend himſelf againſt the enemies' knives. At the ſame time, three children by the name of Allen, all of whom are ſtill living, were purſued ; Eunice, one of the three, was ſtruck down with a tomahawk, which was ſunk into her head, but by reaſon of the haſte in which the enemy retreated, ſhe was left unſcalped, and afterwards recovered. Caleb, the preſent Mr. Caleb Allen, of Deerfield, made his eſcape ; and Samuel was taken captive, the only priſoner who was taken at this time.* The firing immediately alarmed

* This lad, after a year and nine months, was redeemed. Col. Hawks, who was ſent to Canada for the purpoſe of redeeming captives, after enquiring for the lad, was informed, that he was unwilling to be ſeen, and that he expreſſed great diſſatisfaction upon hearing of his arrival : When he

alarmed the town.   Capt. Hopkins, commander of the
standing guard, together with most of the inhabitants, as
volunteers, came on with the utmost expedition, but the
enemy had withdrawn in great haste, expecting, no doubt,
a violent attack; they were pursued several miles by a
body of men, under the command of capt. Cleffon, but
could not be overtaken.

It does not appear, as a matter of certainty, that more
than one of the enemy was killed at this time, and him, by
Samuel Allen; sometime after, however, the remains of a
person were found, near the place of action, supposed to be
those of an Indian.

This was the last mischief, done by the enemy, in the
western frontiers, this season.

April 7, 1747.   A large body of French, and Indians,
appeared at No. 4, and laid siege to the garrison, which
continued for three days, when the enemy withdrew, having done but little damage; only slightly wounding Joseph
Ely, and John Brown.

15th.   Nathaniel Dickinson, and Asahel Burt, of Northfield, being out a little distance from the town, were killed,
and scalped.   The enemy, on their return from Northfield,
burnt most of the buildings in Winchester, and in the upper, and lower Ashwelots, which plantations, a few days
before, had been deserted by the inhabitants, not having
sufficient protection afforded them by government.

May 25.   As fort Massachusetts was rebuilding, there
being several hundred people present, an army of the enemy
came, with a design to hinder the undertaking.   About an
hundred men, a few days before, had been sent to Albany,
for stores of provisions, and ammunition; being on their
return, and near the fort, a scout was sent forward, who,
coming within sight of the fort, discovered the enemy, and
began an attack; this gave an alarm to the people at the
fort,

he was brought into the presence of col. Hawks, he was unwilling to know
him, although he was his uncle, and had always been acquainted with him
in Deerfield; neither would he speak in the English tongue, not that he
had forgotten it, but to express his unwillingness to return; he made use
of various arts, that he might not be exchanged; and finally could not be
obtained but by threats, and was brought off by force.   In this we see the
surprising power of habit; this youth had lost his affection for his country,
and his friends, in the course of one year, and nine months; and had be-
come so attached to the Indians, and their mode of living, as that to this
day, he considers that of the Indians, the happiest life.   This appears
more surprising when we consider, that he fared extremely hard, and was
reduced almost to a skeleton.

fort, who, as yet, had not difcovered the enemy ; a few iffued out, and maintained a fmall fkirmifh, till the enemy withdrew. There was, at the time, much complaint, both of the people at the fort, and of the commander of that party who was with the waggons, for not affording affift-ance, which was imputed to cowardice. In this action, three perfons were wounded ; and a friend Indian, who belonged to Stockbridge, was killed.

July 15. Eliakim Sheldon, of Bernardfton, was fired upon, and wounded ; he died the following night.

The fame month, John Mills, of Colrain, paffing from what was called the fouth fort, to his own houfe, was fired upon and killed.

Auguft 26. A fmall party of the enemy came to a village belonging to Northampton, (now Southampton), and killed, and fcalped, Elijah Clark, as he was threfhing in his barn.

October 1. Peter Burree was taken captive near Maf-fachufetts' fort.

19th. John Smead, as he was travelling from North-field to Sunderland, was killed, and fcalped, near the mouth of Miller's river. He had but a few days before returned from captivity, being one who was taken at Maffachufetts' fort, with his wife, and children.

About this time, Jonathan Sawtel was taken captive, from Hinfdale.

14th. As twelve men were paffing down the river, from No. 4, they were ambufhed, and a fkirmifh enfued ; Nathaniel Gould, and Thomas Goodall, were killed, and fcalped ; Oliver Avery was wounded, and John Henderfon taken captive, the remainder made their efcape.

March 15, 1748. About eight men were out a few rods from the fort, at No. 4, and were attacked by about twenty Indians, who endeavoured to cut off their retreat to the fort ; a fkirmifh enfued, in which Charles Stevens was killed ; a man by the name of Androus was wounded, and Eleazer Prieft was taken captive.

April 12. Jafon Babcock was taken prifoner, being at work in his field, at Poquiag.

May 9. Noah Pixley was killed, and fcalped, at Southampton.

About the fame time, capt. Melvin, with eighteen men, being at the lake, near Crownpoint, fired at two canoes of Indians : On his return, being on Weft river, about 35 miles

miles from fort Dummer, was ambufhed, and being fired on
by furprife, his men were fcattered : Two or three returned
the fire, and killed two of the enemy : The fame perfons,
after having gone fome diftance, and having fallen in company with three or four of their own men, concluded to
return back, and give the enemy a fhot ; on their return
they were fired on, and one was killed ; they returned the
fire, and killed one of the enemy.  The whole company,
excepting fix, made their efcape through the woods, and
came in at different times.  In this fkirmifh, Jofeph Petty,
John Heywood, John Dod, Daniel Mann, and Ifaac Taylor, were killed ; Samuel Severance could not be found,
and was fuppofed to be taken captive.  The lofs of thefe
men, was much lamented ; and they are fpoken of with
refpect, as prudent, virtuous men, and refolute foldiers.

June 16.  As thirteen men were marching from colonel
Hinfdale's, to fort Dummer, they were ambufhed by a
large body of the enemy and were fired upon.  Jofeph
Richardfon, Nathan French, and John Froft, were killed
the firft fhot, and feven were immediately taken captive,
viz. Henry Stevens, Benjamin Ofgood, William Blanchard,
Matthew Wiman, Joel Johnfon, Mofes Perkins, and William Bickford.  Bickford was either killed by the enemy, the
firft night, or had been wounded, and died of his wounds.

26th. Capt. Hobbs, paffing through the woods from
No. 4, to fort Shirley, with forty men, and being about
twelve miles northweft of fort Dummer, was attacked by a
large body of the enemy, who had purfued him ; it being
in the middle of the day, he had made a ftand, that his
men might receive fome refrefhment ; whilft they were
dining, the fcout, which was fent upon the back track,
were fired on.  Upon this, capt. Hobbs put his men into as
much readinefs for an action, as two or three minutes
would admit of.  The enemy came on with great fury,
expecting, no doubt, an immediate furrendry ; but capt.
Hobbs gave them a warm reception, and fought, for four
hours, with fuch boldnefs and fortitude, as that had he,
and his men, been Romans, they would have received a
laurel, and their names would have been handed down with
honour, to the lateft pofterity ; the enemy finally fled in
hafte, and with great lofs.  Capt. Hobbs, in this action,
loft but three men, and had but three wounded ; thofe killed were Ebenezer Mitchel, Eli Scott, and Samuel Gunn.

I.                                                    July

July 14. As a fcout of feventeen men were paffing from col. Hinfdale's to fort Dummer, they were ambufhed, and fired upon, by about 120 of the enemy ; two only were killed the firft fhot ; two more were wounded, and but four made their efcape; the remainder were taken captive ; the wounded the enemy killed, after having carried them about a mile.

23d. The enemy waylaid the main ftreet, at Northfield, and killed Aaron Belding.

Auguft 2. About 200 of the enemy, made their appearance at fort Maffachufetts; the fort was then under the command of capt. Ephraim Williams : A fcout was firft fired upon, which drew out capt. Williams, with about thirty men ; an attack began, which continued for fome time ; but, finding the enemy numerous, capt. Williams fought upon the retreat, till he had again recovered the fort : The enemy foon withdrew, and with what lofs was unknown. In this action, one Abbot was killed, lieut. Hawley, and Ezekiel Wells were wounded, but recovered.

This is the laft account I can find, of mifchief done by the enemy in the weftern frontiers, in what is called the firft French war. Peace, however, was not finally fettled with the Indians, until October 1749, when a treaty was held at Falmouth, by commiffioners from the General Court, and the chiefs of the Indian tribes, by whom a former treaty, with fome additions, was renewed.

Peace between France and England, took place in the year 1748, and war was again declared in 1756 ; but, in the fummer of 55, a body of Indians appeared at Stockbridge, killed feveral perfons, and did confiderable mifchief, in killing cattle, &c.

In June, the fame fummer, a number of perfons being at work in the meadow, at the upper part of Charlemont, were fired on by a party of the enemy ; not fo much mifchief was done, as might have been expected ; a number made their efcape : Cap. Rice, and Phinehas Arms, were killed, their bodies were afterwards found in a mangled condition. Titus King, and a lad, were taken captive.

The fame month, capt. Bridgman's fort, at Hinfdale, was taken by ftratagem, and a number of perfons were captivated. It was fuppofed that the enemy had been lurking about for fome time, and the fituation of the fort was fuch as that whatever paffed, either in, or near it, might

might be eafily feen from the hills a little back : It was the cuftom of the fort, for the women within to faften the gate when the men went into the fields to labour, and to open it upon their return, from the fignal of knocking : The Indians obferving this, took an opportunity when the men were at the greateft diftance from the fort, came, and knocked at the gate ; and the women, being under no fpecial apprehenfions of an enemy, immediately threw open the gate, when, to their aftonifhment, they found the enemy entering ; no refiftance was made in the fort, and fourteen perfons were taken captive. The enemy made no longer tarry at the fort, than to fecure the prifoners, but rufhed into the meadow, and fell upon the men, who, as yet, had not difcovered what had paffed at the fort ; they made as much refiftance as their fituation would admit of. In this fkirmifh, C. Howe was killed, the remainder made their efcape.

About this time, the fort at Keene, under the command of capt. Sims, was attacked by a large party of Indians, and with great fury ; the attack was lengthy, but was fuftained with fortitude. The enemy finding their attempts to take the fort ineffectual, gave over the attack, but wreaked their vengeance on the inhabitants, by deftroying all the property they could find, in killing cattle, burning buildings, &c. In this fiege, no lives were loft, and but one perfon was taken captive, he being out of the fort at the time.

July 3. The enemy appeared at Keene, and captivated a perfon by the name of Frizzle.

-The fame month, fort Hinfdale was attacked by a confiderable body of the enemy. In this attack two perfons were killed, and one was taken captive ; one of the perfons killed was John Alexander.

About the fame time, two men were killed, at Bellows's fort. Alfo, a man, by the name of Pike, was killed at fome place up the river, but where I cannot tell.

June 7, 1756. Jofiah Fofter, with his family, were taken captive, at Winchefter. The fame day, a body of the enemy appeared at fort Maffachufetts. Benjamin King, and a man by the name of Meacham, were killed.

The fame month, lieut. Jofeph Willard, was killed at No. 4.

On the 25th, as a number of men were coming from the army at the lake, they were attacked by a large body of the enemy, and it is probable that a fevere action enfued, tho' I cannot afcertain the particulars ; there were, however, eight men killed, and five taken captive.                    July

July 11. The enemy came to Weft Hoofick, and killed capt. Chapin, and two perfons by the name of Chidefter.

Auguft 12, 1756. A party of five, or fix Indians, made their appearance in Deerfield, (now Greenfield), at a place called the country farms ; feveral men, viz. Benjamin Haftings, John Graves, Daniel Graves, Nathaniel Brooks, and Shubal Atherton, being at work, were furprifed, by difcovering the enemy between them and their guns, and being in no fituation to make any refiftance, found no way to fave themfelves, but by flight. They had fled but a few rods, before they were fired on ; none were either killed, or wounded the firft fhot ; the enemy ftill purfued, and continued their firing. Shubal Atherton was foon killed ; Benjamin Haftings, and John Graves, made their efcape ; Daniel Graves, and Nathaniel Brooks, were taken captive. Graves was killed, after the enemy had conveyed him but a little diftance ; he was in years, and it was fuppofed, he was unable to travel with fuch fpeed as the enemy wifhed. Brooks never returned from his captivity.

1757. The enemy appeared at No. 4, and captivated five perfons ; the particulars of this matter I cannot afcertain.

March 20, 1758. J. Morrifon, and J. Henry of Colrain, being near what is called north river, (a branch of Deerfield river), were fired on, and were both wounded ; capt. Morrifon's barn was burnt, and his cattle were killed the fame day.

March 21, 1759. The enemy again appeared at Colrain, and captivated Jofeph M'Ewers, with his wife. Mrs. M'Ewers, was killed by the enemy, after one day's travel, fhe being unable to proceed.

This is the laft account, which I can obtain, of mifchief done by the enemy, in the weftern frontiers, in the laft French war.

APPREHENDING that it will not be difagreeable to the publick, I here fubjoin a circumftantial account of what is called the *fall fight*, which happened in May, 1676.

The following, I have taken in part, from Hubbard's hiftory of the Indian wars ; but principally from an attefted copy of a manufcript, written by fome gentlemen who were in the action.

Several large bodies of Indians had affembled at different places about Deerfield. Two tribes had feated themfelves at the falls, one on the eaft, and the other on the weft fide

of

of the river.  A little below the falls, upon an ifland, was
another tribe.  Another had placed themfelves on the weft
fide of the river, at a little diftance above the falls : And a
fifth had taken their refidence at Cheapfide.

These Indians, being previoufly informed, by fome of
their captives, that the forces were principally withdrawn
from the neighbouring towns, had imprudently fallen into
a ftate of unguarded fecurity.  The inhabitants being informed of this, by fome prifoners, who had been fo fort-
unate as to make their efcape, determined to improve the
opportunity, and if poffible, extirpate them from this part
of the country.  All the foldiers, who could be raifed, for
this almoft defperate expedition, both from the militia, and
the ftanding forces, amounted to only one hundred and
fixty.  The ftanding forces were commanded by capt.
Turner, of Bofton.  The volunteers by their own officers.
Thofe from Springfield, by capt. Holyoke ; from Northampton, by enfign Lyman ; from Hadley, and Hatfield, by
fergeants Kellogg, and Dickinfon.  The Rev. Hope
Atherton, minifter of the gofpel, at Hatfield, a gentleman
of publick fpirit, accompanied the army.  The pilots were
meffrs. Benjamin Wait, and Experience Hinfdale.

Thefe troops marched from Hatfield May 17, 1676, a
little before night.  Paffing Deerfield river, at Cheapfide,
they were heard by the Indian fentinel, who immediately
alarmed the tribe, informing them, that horfes had paffed
the river.  Search was immediately made, at the ufual
fording place, which our troops had happily miffed, having
by miftake, croffed a little above, and the enemy finding
no tracks, concluded, that their fentry had been deceived,
and that what he heard, muft have been the noife of moofe,
paffing the river near the fording place.  Meeting with no
oppofition from this tribe, our troops marched on, till they
came to the falls.  It was now about the break of day.
According to their wifhes, our army found the enemy in
an unguarded fituation, without even a fentinel.  The reafon
why, at this time, they were thus furprifingly unguarded,
was, the evening before they had been rioting upon milk,
and roaft beef, having been pillaging cows from the neighbouring towns.  When the day opened, fo that our army
could diftinguifh friends from foes, they marched up and
began the attack, by firing into the wigwams.  The Indians awaking in furprife, and in their confternation fup-

L 2                                    poling

pofing that they were attacked by their native enemies, cried, Mohawks ! Mohawks ! They foon, however, dif-covered their miftake ; but being in no fituation to make an immediate defence, great numbers were flain upon the fpot, fome, in their furprife, ran directly into the river, and were drowned ; others betook themfelves to their baık canoes, and having in their confufion forgot their paddles, were hurried down the falls, and dafhed againft the rocks ; and many who had endeavoured to fecrete themfelves under the river banks, were difcovered, and flain.

In this action the enemy, by their own confeffion, loft 300, women, and children included.

This victory, though great, and obtained with the lofs of only one man, in the firft onfet, was yet, howeve, difaft-rous in the iffue. The few who had not been flain, of this tribe, after recovering from their fright, and being joined by the neighbouring tribes, difcovering the fmallnefs of the number, by whom they had been thus furioufly attacked, and by whom they had fuftained fuch a lofs, purfued, and harraffed the army on their retreat, with fuch fury, that thirty-feven were killed, and feveral were wounded.

This lofs was imputed, in part, to the bodily infirmities of capt. Turner ; and in part to the want of ammunition, which was the caufe of an ill-timed and unguarded retreat.

A few, to the number of about twenty, did not quit the ground, with the main body of the army, but tarried be-hind, for the purpofe of firing at fome of the enemy who were croffing the river. Thefe men foon found themfelves under the neceffity of difputing the ground, with a confid-erable body of the enemy, before they could recover their horfes ; but after a fevere fkirmifh, obtained their object, and foon came up with the army, which was furrounded, and fought on their retreat for ten miles. Seven, or eight men, in the beginning of the retreat, were, by fome acci-dent, unfortunately feparated from the army, and foon found themfelves loft. The Indians afterwards gave the following account of them : That on Monday after the fight, eight Englifhmen came to them, who were loft, and offered to furrender, on condition their lives might be fpared ; but, inftead of giving them quarter, they took and burnt them in the following manner :—They firft covered them with dry thatch, then fet fire to it, and compelled them to run : When one covering was burnt off, they put

on

on another, and fo continued, till death delivered them from their hands.

This expedition was productive of very happy confequences, for the enemy were fo difconcerted in all their plans, and fo greatly difheartened, that they never after, during that war, gave any confiderable difturbance to the frontiers. From this expedition may be dated their decline in thefe parts.

In the above action was one Jonathan Wells, of Hatfield, then a youth in his 17th year, he was afterwards a gentleman improved in publick life, and fuftained a worthy character. The following is the fubftance of an attefted copy of the account, taken from his own mouth.

Mr. Wells was one of the 20 men abovementioned, who were under a neceffity of difputing the ground, for the purpofe of recovering their horfes. Soon after he had mounted, being in the rear, three of the enemy fired upon him ; one of their balls brufhed his hair, another wounded his horfe, and a third ftruck his thigh, in a place where it had before been broken with a cart wheel ; the ball did not wholly break his thigh anew, but fractured the end of one of the bones, which was a little projected over the other, it having been badly fet. Upon receiving the wound, it was with difficulty that Mr. Wells kept in his faddle. The Indians perceiving they had wounded him, preffed hard upon him. Mr. Wells, recovering a little from the firft fhock, and perceiving the enemy almoft upon him, prefented his gun, which gave them a check, and whilft they were charging, he made his efcape, and reached the company. He reprefented to capt. Turner, the danger to which the people in the rear were expofed, and urged him to return to their relief, or halt till they might come up ; but he anfwered, " It is better to lofe fome, than all." The army was now divided into feveral companies, one pilot crying, " If you will fave your lives, follow me ;" and another, " If you regard your fafety, follow me." Mr. Wells was now following a company, whofe courfe was towards a fwamp ; but perceiving that a body of the enemy were there, he left that company, who were all loft, and joined a fmall party, who were taking a different route ; but his horfe foon failing by reafon of his wound, and himfelf being much weakened by lofs of blood, he was left by this party, having only one Jones, a wounded man to accompany him : They had no path to guide them,

and

and were both unacquainted with the woods. They had
not travelled far, before Mr. Wells was separated from Jones,
and finding himself faint, eat a nutmeg which he had in his
pocket, upon which he revived. After having wandered
in the woods for some time, he came upon green river, and
he followed the course of it up, till he came to a place called the country farms ; having passed the river he attempted to ascend a mountain on the west side, but fainted, and
fell from his horse.✳ How long he lay in this condition he
knew not, but when he recovered, he found his horse
standing by him, and his bridle hanging on his hand. He
arose, tied his horse, and again laid himself down ; but upon
reflection, finding himself already so weak as to be unable
to mount, concluded that he should have no farther use for
his horse, and being unwilling he should die at the tree, dis-
missed him ; but unhappily forgot to take any provision
from his portmanteau, although it contained a plenty.
Towards night, being troubled with musquetoes, he struck
up a fire ; but this almost proved his destruction ; it arose,
and spread with such fury, among the leaves and trash, that
it was with difficulty, in his faint condition, he escaped
perishing in the flames.✳ After he was out of danger, from
the fire, he again laid himself down to rest ; but now new
fears arose ; he imagined that the fire would direct the enemy where to find him ; and serve to betray him into their
hands : Unwilling the enemy should be benefited by his
ammunition, he cast it to as great a distance as he could,
reserving only a charge or two for their use, should he fall
into their hands. After some time, finding his fire had
spread considerably, he took courage, put some tow into
his wounds, bound them up with his handkerchief, and
composed himself to sleep. In his sleep he dreamed, that
his grandfather came to him, and told him he was lost, and
must turn, and go down that river, till he should come to
the end of a mountain, where he would find a plain, upon
whic' he must travel, in order to find his way home.
When he awoke he found himself refreshed, his bleeding
stopped, and his strength recruited, and with the help of
his gun as a staff, he was able to walk, though but slowly.
The rising of the sun, convinced him, he was lost, and that
the course he intended to pursue was wrong. He had now
wandered six or seven miles farther from home, than when
he set out from the place of action. And though, at first,
                                                        he

he paid no attention to his dream, now he determined to follow the directions of it. Accordingly, he travelled down the river, found the end of the mountain, and soon came to the plain ; all of which, agreed to the representation in his dream.* Soon after he entered upon the plain, he found a foot path, which led him to the road, in which, the main body of the army returned. When he came to Deerfield river, he met with much difficulty in crossing ; the stream carrying his lame leg across the other, so that several of his first attempts were without effect. Finally, however, with the help of his gun, with much difficulty he reached the opposite shore. When he had ascended the bank, being greatly fatigued, he laid himself down under a walnut bush, and fell asleep. When he awoke, the first object that presented, was an Indian in a canoe, coming directly towards him. Mr. Wells now found himself in a very unhappy condition, being so disabled by his wounds that he could not flee, and his gun being so filled with gravel and sand, in crossing the river, that he could not fight. So soon however, as he perceived the Indian had discovered him, he presented his gun, which so affrighted him, that he leaped out of the canoe, leaving his own gun, and made his escape. Mr. Wells concluding that he would inform the whole tribe, who were only a few rods distant, went into a neighbouring swamp, and finding two logs lying near each other, and covered over with rubbish, he crept between them. He soon heard the noise of Indians ; but was not curious to look out after them. When the noise had ceased, he ventured to proceed forward. In Deerfield meadow he found some horses' bones, from which he scraped some matter, which served for food ; he also found two or three rotten beans, where the Indians had threshed, and also two blue-bird's eggs, which was all the sustenance he had till he reached home. He came to Deerfield town plat, on Saturday

* I doubt, whether, in this dream, there was any thing supernatural, as some may be ready to suppose. Mr. Wells, having wandered in the woods six or seven miles, must necessarily have had some doubts whether his course was right ; and his mind, when asleep, would more naturally employ itself on this subject, than any other ; because to find the way home, must have been his great object, when awake. His dreaming that his grandfather appeared to him, was nothing strange ; and his local situation at this time was such, that he could not be entirely unacquainted with the natural make of the ground ; and his thoughts running as they did, in this dream, would be natural ; the river was near him—the plain was before him—and the end of the mountain, near the side of the plain, if he had not previously seen it, would naturally be supposed.

day night about dark, but as there were no inhabitants
prefent, the town having a little before been burnt, he continued his courfe in the evening.

He was often under great difcouragements, and frequently laid himfelf down to die, expecting to rife no more.   He
reached no farther than muddy brook as the fun rofe on
Sabbath morning.   Here, feeing a human head, which had
been dug up by wild beafts, Mr. Wells, notwithftanding the
diftreffes of his condition, ftopped to find the grave, which
having found he laid the head to the body, and covered it
with billets of wood, to defend it from the ravenous beafts
of the wildernefs.   After he had left the brook and entered upon the plain, he grew faint and very thirfty, but could
obtain no water for a confiderable time ; he was, however,
often refrefhed, by holding his face in the fmoke of burning
knots of pine, which he frequently met with, as the woods
were on fire.   Mr. Wells arrived at Hatfield on the Sabbath, between meetings, and was received with inexpreffible
joy, as one having arifen from the dead.   He endured in-
credible pain, and diftrefs, with his wound, being confined
feveral times to his bead, for fix months together ; and it
was upwards of four years before he was found.

In this action was alfo the Rev. Mr. Atherton, minifter
of the gofpel, in Hatfield.   The following is the fubftance
of a paragraph, which he delivered to his people the Sabbath after his return :

" In the hurry and confufion of the retreat, I was feparated from the army ; the night following, I wandered up
and down among the dwelling places of the enemy, but
none of them difcovered me.   The next day, I tendered
myfelf to them a prifoner, for no way of efcape appeared,
and I had been a long time without food ; but notwithftanding I offered myfelf to them, yet, they accepted not
the offer ; when I fpake they anfwered not ; and when I
moved toward them they fled.*   Finding they would not accept of me as a prifoner, I determined to take the courfe of
the river and if poffible find the way home, and after feveral
days of hunger, fatigue and danger, I reached Hatfield."

*Deerfield, October* 10th, 1793.

*The*

* There were various conjectures at the time, relative to this ftrange conduct of the Indians ; the moft probable one was, that it arofe from fome of
their religious fuperftitions.

*The following observations were added by* Mr. T. PRINCE, *to the third edition, for the information of our younger people.*

THE reverend author of the preceeding hiſtory and ſermon was a ſon of Mr. Samuel Williams, of Roxbury, where he was born Dec. 10, 1664 ; took his firſt degree at Harvard college in 1683 ; was ordained the firſt paſtor of the church in Deerfield, in May, 1686.

And his firſt wife Eunice, murdered by the barbarous Indians, as before related, was the only daughter of the Rev. Mr. Eleazer Mather, firſt paſtor of the church in Northampton, by his only wife, Mrs. Eſther, the daughter of the reverend and famous Mr. John Warham, formerly a miniſter in Exeter, in England, who came to New-England in 1630, was the firſt teacher with the Rev. Mr. Maverick, paſtor of the firſt church in Dorcheſter, near Boſton ; and in 1635, removed, with the greater part of his church, to Windſor, on Connecticut river, where he continued their paſtor until he died. After the Rev. Mr. Eleazer Mather's death, his widow married the Rev. Mr. Solomon Stoddard, who ſucceeded him in the paſtoral office at Northampton.

When Deerfield was deſtroyed, in February, 1703-4, it was in the firſt year of my living at Harvard college ; and I well remember how generally and greatly affected were the good people of this province, with that terrible diſaſter.

His eldeſt ſon, Eleazer, being then in another town, eſcaped that calamity. The next commencement, by the encouragement and help of divers charitable people, eſpecially in Boſton, he entered Harvard college ; and living in the chamber over me, I fell into an intimate acquaintance with him ; and found him a perſon of eminent piety, humility, ſincerity, and ſweetneſs of temper, like his father. He took his firſt degree in 1708, and became the faithful paſtor of the church in Mansfield in Connecticut, until he died.

His reverend father returning from captivity, and arriving at Boſton, November 21, 1706, to the great joy of the people ; and being informed that he was to preach the publick lecture there on December 6th, I, with many others, went down, and in an auditory exceedingly crowded and affected, I heard the ſermon herewith reprinted. And in thoſe times, there was ſuch a tender union, affection, and chriſtian ſimplicity, among the good people here, that, as
the

the apoftle lively defcribes it, ' When one member of the ' fociety fuffered, the whole body feemed to fuffer with it ; ' and when one rejoiced, the whole rejoiced.'

By the like kind encouragement, the Rev. Mr. Williams had his fon Stephen Williams educated at Harvard college ; who took his firft degree in 1713 ; was ordained paftor of a church in Springfield ; and is fo extenfively known and valued, that his name only need to be mentioned ; as that of his fon Warham—who took his firft degree in 1719, and became the worthy paftor of the church in Waltham, form- erly a part of Watertown ; not long fince deceafed.

The Rev. Mr. Williams, of Deerfield, ufed every May, yearly, to come down to the general convention of the min- ifters of the province at Bofton ; where he was always very affectionately entertained.

At the convention in May, 1728, (being chofen the year before) he preached a very moving fermon to the minifters ; when I remember, he expreffed his joy in the great advan- tage we at that time had above the preceeding minifters, in the general awakenings through the land, by the great earthquake in October foregoing. And on June 12, 1729, he died, greatly beloved and lamented.

And by the accounts above, we may learn, from the in- ftance of this one town only in our weftern frontiers of the province of the Maffachufetts bay, in New-England, what horrible murders and defolations this province has fuffered from the French and Indians in all our wars with them ever fince the year 1675, when the Indians firft broke out upon us—and what numbers of the prefent people in Canada are the children of this province, or defcendants from them— which, in cafe the fovereign God fhould ever lead a victorious army of ours into Canada, will clearly juftify us to all the world, if we fhould bring every child and defcendant of New- England, yea of all the Britifh colonies, away—efpecially confidering we fhould bring them into a much pleafanter and more plenteous land and agreeable climate ; out of a wretched land of darknefs and flavery, both religious and civil, into a land of glorious light and liberty. And may the Almighty haften it in his time !

T. PRINCE.

*Bofton, Dec.* 20, 1757.

*F I N I S.*